29-11

THE PRESIDENTS

AND THE PRESS

TRUMAN TO JOHNSON

By James E. Pollard

Public Affairs Press, Washington, D. C.

FOREWORD

After ten years in preparation, *The Presidents and the Press* was published in 1947. This was the first work in which the relations between the Presidents from George Washington through Franklin D. Roosevelt were recounted and analyzed in detail. This book has now been out of print for some years.

Between 1951 and the winter of 1964, the author wrote seven supplementary articles dealing with the same central theme. One of these was published in the Winter 1951-52 issue of the *Public Opinion Quarterly*. The six others appeared in the *Journalism Quarterly*, two having to do with the Truman news relations, three with those under Mr. Eisenhower, and one with those of Mr. Kennedy. In September, 1945, also, a brief article on Franklin D. Roosevelt's press relations appeared in the *Journalism Quarterly*, but these were dealt with at length in the book.

The first seven articles referred to above are brought together in this small monograph, plus a brief new chapter dealing with the Johnson administration. The articles are unchanged even though they overlap to some extent. Permission to republish them in this form, as a kind of supplement to the original book, has been given by the *Public Opinion Quarterly* and the *Journalism Quarterly*.

Because of the tremendous advances in news coverage, particularly through radio and television, the relationship between the executive branch of the government, especially the White House and the news media, has taken on added importance since the death of Franklin D. Roosevelt in April, 1945. From the standpoint of an informed public, the developments traced herein are far more significant than those of the preceding thirty years.

JAMES E. POLLARD

Ohio State University
Columbus, Ohio

3

CONTENTS

I

HISTORICAL PERSPECTIVE

Relations of one kind or another between the Presidents and the press have existed from the time of George Washington to that of Lyndon B. Johnson. It is a very long way, both in time and in the nature of that relationship, between the first and the thirty-sixth Presidents. The beginnings, in fact, are somewhat obscure but they are there in the pro- and anti-administration organs, in personal correspondence, and in other ways.

The Presidential news conference, now taken for granted as a highly important device, had its real origins in the first administration of Woodrow Wilson. For two reasons this turned out to be a relatively brief experiment. One was that Wilson soon became annoyed and angered at what he felt was the unjustified prying of the newsmen into the private affairs of the Presidential family, especially of the three Wilson daughters. The other was the growing involvement of the United States in critical foreign affairs, first with the onset of war in Europe and then with Mexico. This took more and more of Wilson's time and energy. By the very nature of this stern and difficult man it is doubtful whether the attempt at regular news conferences would have lasted anyway.

The news conferences were renewed under Warren G. Harding, himself a newspaper editor and publisher of long standing. Despite this supposedly favorable climate they were not particularly successful. In any case, he died after only twenty-nine months of an administration already scarred by the growing revelations of widespread scandal and corruption. For his successor, Calvin Coolidge, the claim has been made that he held more news conferences than any other President. This is highly debatable both as to definition and actual number. In any case, by the first-hand testimony of Washington correspondents of that day, the Coolidge news conferences were as dull and generally unproductive as the man himself.

Franklin D. Roosevelt gave new status, continuity and color to the news conferences. His four-term administration, unprecedented in itself, was a "new deal" for the Washington correspondents as well as for the country. He had to deal with a massive economic depression followed by direct American involvement in the most far-flung and bloodiest war the world had ever known. Yet in his twelve years-plus in office, he somehow found the time and the energy to hold 998 news conferences. Generally there were two a week. His innovation of the "fireside chats" was, in effect, an extension of his effective and successful use of the news conference as a major means of communication with the American public.

At his very first White House news conference he banned written questions and laid down rules as to background and off-the-record information. He often supplemented the news of the moment or previewed that to come with significant material and information not to be ascribed to him.

Mr. Truman was of a different stripe. Both he and his predecessor were on rather familiar terms with the correspondents, but each developed his own methods. If anything, Mr. Truman was saltier and more homespun in his responses than Mr. Roosevelt had been. In the main, however, he continued and expanded the methods used by the latter.

A major development of the later Truman years was the rapid growth of television as a direct means of communication. His news conferences were relatively less frequent than those under Mr. Roosevelt. Television figured inevitably in what might be called a visual extension of the "fireside chat" device.

Jointly the radio and television of necessity rather quickly brought about a change in the handling of news and in the makeup of those in attendance at the White House news room and at the Presidential news conferences. The public could now begin to see and hear, at first hand, what the President said, and how he looked and acted on those occasions. But for a more detailed and tangible account of what was said and done, the public was still dependent largely upon the press, including the news magazines. In fairness to all the media, it must be conceded that each offered certain advantages in bringing the Presidential image close to the people.

Mr. Eisenhower had a different personality from those of either the two men who preceded him or the two who followed him in such close order. Not long before he took office there was momentary doubt as to whether he would continue the news conferences. But he soon dispelled this by announcing that he would do so. So they were continued during his eight years, with some further modifications in the interest of the correspondents, the media they represented, and the ultimate public.

As President, Mr. Eisenhower bore something of the "father" image and this was reflected to a degree in his news conferences. While he knew some correspondents fairly well he was hardly on a familiar or easy footing with them. It is doubtful whether he enjoyed his news conferences; rather, they were something to be endured. On a number of occasions he was obviously annoyed by questions and had difficulty maintaining his composure. Subject to editing, he permitted direct quotation and the use of television.

Mr. Kennedy and Mr. Johnson were something else. The former was young, outwardly jovial and convivial, quick in his responses, and always with the ready word or fact in reply to a question. Only fifteen years before entering the White House he had been briefly a member of the working press and knew something of its day-to-day needs and requirements at first hand. During his years in the House and the Senate he had come to know quite a few of the correspondents on a personal, man-to-man and man-to-politician basis. Some of these relationships he continued during his brief time in the White House. Whether by design or otherwise, it might even be said that he excelled in personal contacts with the news media, often directly but also indirectly through others.

During the thirty-four months of the Kennedy incumbency, Lyndon Johnson remained in the background. Publicly, for the most part, he kept his mouth shut and his ideas to himself. From protocol and from necessity he remained in the wings, ready to do the President's bidding but otherwise merely the silent Number Two man in the administration.

Then on that tragic early afternoon of November 22, 1963 all this was changed. Within a matter of minutes, Mr. Johnson boarded Air Force One, was sworn into office and, with characteristic vigor, gave the order to get airborne and the Presidential party was on its way back to Washington. The first thing the new chief executive did on his arrival at Andrews Air Force Base, outside the capital, was to go before the microphones and television cameras for a brief message to the public. This had already been made available to the few news men aboard Air Force One.

Even before the Kennedy obsequies were completed, President Johnson moved rapidly. He consulted with Mr. Truman and Mr. Eisenhower. He talked with the heads or representatives of other governments who had come to Washington for the Kennedy funeral. Very quickly he made himself available to the correspondents, especially the White House "regulars" most of whom he already knew to some extent. So just as there was only a momentary interruption in the Presidential office, there was no break in contacts between the President and the news media. There was every sign that this expanding channel begun in earnest in 1913 would not only be continued but enlarged.

II

THE WHITE HOUSE AS NEWS SOURCE

The government of the United States was far more remote from the people when the nation was young and confined to a narrow strip of seaboard than it is now, when it stretches from sea to sea and when its population has grown forty-fold. But this is easily explained by both the political and the physical conditions of the time. The government of 1789 was not a truly popular government and had little direct contact with the public.

Even so elementary a service as reporting the news of the early Congress by the newspapers was unheard of. It was years before they were permitted to have their own reporters cover the sessions. By today's standards, the other branches of government were practically untouchable so far as access by the press was concerned. The executive in particular was remote from the public, and except for proclamations, formal messages, reports and other official utterances, the press and the public were largely dependent upon second-hand sources and rumors for information about that branch of government. The courts, then as now, were aloof from the public, although in time the presence of the press came to be tolerated.

Political parties as well as individual politicians maintained their partisan organs. From the time of Jefferson the organ of the administration in power spoke for it, and other newspapers took their cue from that organ. Even in Lincoln's time some believed that Colonel John W. Forney, publisher of the Washington *Chronicle* and the Philadelphia *Press*, was his mouthpiece. But while Forney undoubtedly had Lincoln's ear at times, he was far from being the administration spokesman that Francis P. Blair had been for Jackson.

The secrecy which cloaked the early doings of Congress had its historical precedent in the fact that the British press was long denied the right to report what went on in Parliament. While some reporters were present at the first session of the House of Representatives in 1789, their attendance was forbidden at the next session. Later, when Samuel Harrison Smith sought permission to report the debates from within the bar, he was turned down. At the next session, however, the speaker was directed to assign places for reporters and stenographers.[1] The Congressional press galleries have become so well established and

11

so valuable a part of the communications machinery that it is difficult to conceive of their being done away with. In practice, the correspondents themselves pass upon the qualifications of those who are admitted. It has been years since either House interfered with these arrangments, and they now have the force and sanction of long practice and tradition.

The Presidency is something else. Almost from the beginning the Presidents have had some dealings with the press. A few, like Jackson, made effective use of it to their own purposes. Most of them suffered from it as critic, or foe, or both. A very few, like Lincoln, got along tolerably well with individual newspaper men, although they, too, suffered from the excesses of the press. The White House as such, however, was off limits to the working press.

It was not until the time of Theodore Roosevelt that a start was made in the direction of organized presidential press relations. There was little improvement under Taft and it was left to Woodrow Wilson to set up regular press conferences. The importance of this development is not detracted from either by the fact that the unbending Wilson was unfitted for the give-and-take of these conferences, or by the fact that the early involvement of the United States in World War I put an end to them.

The White House press conference reached its peak under Franklin D. Roosevelt. Certainly no other President approached him for the number, the scope, the drama or the flavor of his utilization of this device. It would be difficult to calculate the total effect of his news conferences in terms of the political information they yielded, their play upon the forces of public opinion, or their contribution to the shaping of national and international policy; but the net effect would certainly be considerable. Nowhere else in the world does the head of a sovereign state freely and voluntarily subject himself to all manner of newspaper questions, the answer to any one of which may have far-reaching effects.

Time and space do not permit details, but a capsule summary of the White House press conference from 1913 to the present would run something as follows:

Wilson's conferences were fragmentary and unpromising, but important because they gave a regular status to the relationship.

Harding was cordial but his conferences were marred by errors.

Coolidge went through the motions of the conference but his news conferences were rarely fruitful.

Hoover began on good terms with the correspondents but ended on a very sour note.

Roosevelt was unsurpassed in the uses to which he put the device or in his skill in managing it. The effectiveness of the meetings was, however, marred somewhat by his tendency to use the press as a whipping boy.

Truman was runner-up to Roosevelt in his use of the press conference although on a lesser scale; he began on a note of humility that changed to cocksureness after the election of 1948 and tended to waspishness in 1950-51.

A President of the United States has continually at his disposal more than a score of means of communication with the public. These may be either formal of informal. They will vary in "weight" according to circumstances, and an off-hand remark at a presidential news conference may produce wider repercussions than a formal state paper.

Presidents Franklin D. Roosevelt and Truman have enjoyed far greater facilities for communicating information and shaping public opinion than have any of their predecessors. The importance of this fact was magnified by the emergence, between 1933 and 1951, of the White House as one of the two principal centers where world opinion is made. This was due to the severe economic depression of the 1930's and the involvement of the United States in World War II. Following this were the critical developments of the post-war years: the founding of the United Nations, the stalemate over Germany, the occupation of Japan, and, finally, the outbreak of undeclared war in Korea. All this has made Washington and Moscow the major news centers of the post-war world. It has also given tremendous weight to the slightest whisper from the White House, and, as event after event has proven, the repercussions from that sounding board have often been vastly different from what was intended or desired.

A list of the more obvious channels and devices available to the President for communicating with the American public, and indirectly with the world at large, would include the following:

1. Formal messages, such as the State of the Union message of January 8, 1951.
2. Special messages, like the one of April 3, 1950 asking Congress to correct the farm price-support program.
3. Proclamations, such as that of December 16, 1950 declaring a national emergency.
4. White House announcements or statements, such as that of Jan-

uary 31, 1950 that the President had ordered the Atomic Energy Commission to proceed with work on the hydrogen bomb.

5. Official memos to executive officers, like that of January 17, 1951 directing them to adhere to the national manpower mobilization policy.

6. Talks with Congressional leaders, followed by statements like that of December 13, 1950 relative to proclaiming a national emergency.

7. Statements issued following other White House meetings.

8. Statements by executive officers by direction of the White House or with its approval, such as that by Secretary Acheson of January 5, 1950 relative to the then hands-off policy re Formosa.

9. Presidential speaking tours, such as that of May, 1950 to the Pacific Northwest.

10. Special local addresses, such as Mr. Truman's University of Missouri commencement address of June 9, 1950.

11. Addresses before groups meeting in Washington, such as his talk of April 21, 1950 before the American Society of Newspaper Editors.

12. Issuance of executive orders, such as that of January 24, 1951 setting up the Commission on Internal Security and Individual Rights.

13. Statements or disclosures by White House callers, such as Mr. Truman's comment of December 14, 1950 to a radio group that he was handicapped by "living the lives of two men. . ."

14. Release of letters to Congressional leaders on pending matters.

15. Exchange of correspondence with other persons released by the White House.

16. Exchange of telegrams with officials and others, like that of March 21, 1951 with Defense Secretary Marshall that since the start of the fighting in Korea the U.S. had doubled its armed forces.

17. Disclosure of presidential letters, like that of August 29, 1950 to Rep. Gordon L. McDonough (R., Calif.), criticizing the Marine Corps for having "a propaganda machine almost equal to Stalin's."

18. Fireside Chats by radio and television, like that of October 17, 1950 from San Francisco following his conference with Gen. MacArthur.

19. Live, limited radio broadcasts for the annual Red Cross and Community Fund appeals.

20. Special, limited radio broadcasts by transcription, like that of September 28, 1950 urging the election of a Congress "free of petty politics."
21. Regular news conferences, normally held once a week.
22. Special news conferences, like the one at 1 a.m., April 11, 1951 to announce the dismissal of Gen MacArthur.
23. Statements, announcements, etc., attributed to the President's press secretary, like that of March 20, 1950 stating that Secretary Acheson still had the President's complete confidence and would remain as secretary.
24. Replies to questions posed to the White House through the President's press secretary.
25. Unofficial reports and rumors attributed to "an administration lieutenant who asked not to be quoted by name," or "President Truman, it was learned today," or "Legislators who conferred with Mr. Truman said. . ."

Normally, perhaps no more than half a dozen of these channels are likely to be fraught with special importance. But any of them, through intended announcement or accidential disclosure, may convey information having a tremendous impact on national and world politics and upon broad segments of public opinion. Regardless of which channel of communication the President uses on a given occasion, the ultimate —and usually the immediate—media by which what he has to say reaches the public are the press and the radio. Earlier, it was chiefly the newspapers and, to some extent, certain magazines which kept the public informed as to what the White House said and did. Since about the time Franklin Roosevelt first became President, this has been complemented by radio reporting and commentary so that the two now go hand in hand. Accredited radio news men are admitted to the White House news conferences as freely as are accredited newspaper correspondents.

The White House news conference, in particular, has come to have great importance as a means of communication not only between the President and the people but between the United States and the world. That it is extra-legal and exists and continues at the pleasure of the President does not lessen its importance. Having been so long established as a fairly regular White House operation, it is unlikely that any future President could do away with it permanently.

This assertion is borne out by the fact that Franklin D. Roosevelt held his news conferences with relatively few interruptions during his twelve years in office and during the greatest war the world has ever seen. In that time, despite tremendous demands upon him, he held 998 news conferences. Where his predecessor normally held two such conferences a week, President Truman has usually held only one. In his first six years in office Mr. Truman had 256 news conferences, or proportionately a little more than half as many as Mr. Roosevelt.

In the momentous fifteen months between January 1, 1950 and April 1, 1951, Mr. Truman held forty-five press conferences and made four special broadcasts of the stature of Fireside Chats. Thirty-eight of his news conferences occurred during 1950 and only seven in the first three months of 1951. This period was chosen for analysis and examination because it covered the six months before the military involvement in Korea and the nine months following the beginning of that episode. In terms of domestic confusion and global uncertainty it was one of the most hectic periods in modern American history.

On the basis of what transpired at these news conferences, thirty-six can be labled as important, while several yielded announcements, disclosures, or other major news developments of world-shaking importance. One such announcement occurred shortly before the period examined. This was Mr. Truman's statement at his news conference of September 23, 1949, that Russia had produced an atomic explosion. This was the first official word in the Western world that Russia had succeeded in exploding an atomic bomb, although how the United States obtained this information has never been revealed.

A calendar of the Truman news conferences between January 1, 1950 and March 31, 1951 gives an insight into the vacillation, uncertainty and back-tracking—especially the latter—that marked U.S. domestic and foreign policy during this fateful period. Only the briefest summaries are possible here, but the calendar of the thirty-six more important news conferences which follows tells its own story with respect to the vagaries of U.S. policy.[2]

January 5, 1950—In a prepared statement the President announced a hands-off policy regarding Formosa, without previous consultation with Congress; he refused to answer questions about it; Republicans in Congress charged him with scuttling the bipartisan foreign policy.

January 19, 1950—He still insisted that no coal emergency existed, but said he would act in a crisis; he also affirmed his faith in Maj. Gen. Harry Vaughan despite the sharp criticism of him by a Senate subcommittee for his dealings with the "5 percenters."

February 9, 1950—He asserted that the United States intended to pursue its policies toward the USSR and toward international control of atomic weapons unchanged; he admonished a columnist who asked, "Are you intending to say that public discussion does no good?" with "You needn't put any words in my mouth."

February 16, 1950—Questioned about an exclusive interview given to Arthur Krock of *The New York Times,* he declared that he would give exclusive interviews when he pleased and to whom he pleased; he insisted that he was a free agent and was not going to be censored.

March 2, 1950—He said that he would cooperate wholeheartedly on any proposal that would contribute to world peace but that he would not go to Moscow for any reason; he added that he would be glad to see Premier Stalin in Washington; he was silent on a proposal by Sen. McMahon that the North Atlantic Council meet to unite the Western nations on proposals for atomic control and then seek a U.N. meeting in Moscow.

March 31, 1950—He charged Senate Republicans with trying to sabotage the bipartisan foreign policy and warned that by this action they had been the Kremlin's greatest asset in the cold war; he called the G.O.P. assault on the State Department part of the search for an issue to recapture Congress in November; he said that he was fed up with the "fiasco" in the Senate (the McCarthy charges), and charged them with a desire to return to isolationism.

April 13, 1950—He declared that he had the nation in fine shape and proposed to take credit for it; he said that his first five years as President were rather difficult but the country had more employed than ever before and the most prosperous business set-up it had ever seen; the five post-war years were easier on it than the aftermath of any other U.S. war and he thought that the President could take credit for this; he added that he had ordered a federal crime inquiry.

May 4, 1950—He said that he was not alarmed over the possibility of a shooting war with Russia; he declared that the next year's defense budget would be smaller than the one Congress was then working on, and observed that the cold war situation was better now than in 1944; he said also that he was opposed to ex-President Hoover's proposal that the U.N. be reorganized to exclude Communist countries.

May 18, 1950—In a prepared statement, he indorsed the Schumann plan to pool French and German steel and coal industries; he widened the breach with some Senate Democrats by emphasizing that he did not distinguish between Democrats and Republicans in calling for the ousting of "obstructionists" in Congress; he said that Congress screamed about economy but voted it down; he added that an annual deficit of 5 billions was not alarming; eventually the budget would be balanced but the cold war required heavy expenditures.

May 25, 1950—He said that military expenditures might go up before they went down; he implied that he did not have all the necessary facts and figures when he made his May 4 prediction of a lower military budget; he ruled out a proposal by *The Washington Post* for a Commission on National Security, saying that there was no need for a super-government.

June 1, 1950—In a message, he asked Congress for $1,222,500,000 for foreign military aid, while at his news conference he said that the world was closer to a real permanent peace than it had been for the last five years; he disagreed with a Gallup poll to the effect that a majority of the American people expected war in the next five years.

June 23, 1950—He said, with reference to a bill "authorizing" seventy groups, that the U.S. could not afford a 70-group air force and that forty-eight groups were all it could afford.

(The next day he dedicated the Baltimore airport, then flew home to Independence, Mo. The following day he flew back to Washington because of the Korean crisis.)

June 29, 1950—He declared that Sen. Taft's demand for the resignation of Secretary Acheson was "entirely uncalled for"; he emphasized that the U.S. intended to save the Republic of Korea no matter what had to be done; he had "no comment" on the use of ground forces, the atom bomb or any increase in aircraft and ammunition production because of the crisis; he said that the U.S. was "not at war" and the actions taken were simple "police actions under the U.N."

July 6, 1950—He expressed confidence in the general situation in Korea despite American setbacks; he said that he had no plans to call out the National Guard or to ask Congress for additional military funds.

July 13, 1950—He said that he had under consideration all steps necessary to meet the emergency but emphasized that rationing was not contemplated; he was confident that a foothold could be held right up to the 38th Parallel; he still regarded the action as a police action; asked whether the U.S. was prepared to meet aggression everywhere in the world, he replied that he would have to meet the situation as it developed; he replied similarly when asked whether the action would be carried north of the 38th Parallel.

July 27, 1950—After the House Banking Committee had approved his milder (than Baruch) program of limited economic controls, Mr. Truman told his news conference that he saw no necessity for others and hoped complete mobilization would not be necessary; he disclosed that the administration was putting finishing touches on a 3-year, 12 billion dollar program of military assistance for the Allies, who were to add 8 more billions; whenever it was necessary to impose wage and price controls and manpower allocations, he said that the steps would be taken together.

August 10, 1950—He announced that he was sending a special mission to Japan to see Gen. MacArthur to discuss a Japanese peace treaty, the future of Formosa, U.S. relations with the Chinese Communists, and strengthening Southeast Asia against further Communist encroachment; he defended policies of Secretaries Acheson and Johnson, and denounced the 100 million dollar loan to Spain through the E.C.A.

August 31, 1950—He again gave Secretary Johnson his full backing and denied that he was "embarrassed" by Johnson or that he contemplated any change in the Defense Secretary's job; he said sharply that controversy over a MacArthur statement was a closed incident; he would not say whether he intended to impound the Spanish loan authorized by Congress, nor would he hazard a guess on the November elections; he again indorsed his Point 4 program; he hoped that the Chinese Communists would stay out of the Korean conflict (military intelligence said two Chinese divisions had moved into position near the Manchurian border); he assailed the refusal of New York and other dock workers to unload Russian goods, and said foreign policy was made at the White House.

September 14, 1950—Reading from a statement prepared by the State Department, he said that he had directed the State Department to start discussions with other nations as to a Japanese peace treaty, Russia or no; he hedged on his earlier statement that he would veto the Communist-control bill passed two days earlier; he again declared firmly that Secretary Acheson would remain and insisted the Johnson incident was closed (Johnson had resigned September 12).

September 21, 1950—He indorsed the statement by Averell Harriman that Senator Taft had furthered "the design of the Kremlin" by his voting record on foreign policy issues, which touched off more protests; he said that crossing the 38th Parallel was up to the U.N.; he declined to say what he would do with the Communist-control (McCarran) bill, but disclosed that price ceilings were under consideration.

September 28, 1950—He declined comment on the Jonathan Daniels report that he had said Byrnes "failed miserably" as Secretary of State, and said that the Daniels book spoke for itself; he named Robert Lovett deputy to Defense Secretary Marshall; he rejoiced over the victories in Korea but warned against a let-up; he said that rearming would go on, that wage and price controls were still under consideration, but was silent on the 38th Parallel, which he said was up to the U.N.

October 19, 1950—He said that he would enforce the new internal security law although he called it pro-Communist; he exploded with anger when asked whether he and Gen. MacArthur were in complete agreement on Formosa (he and MacArthur conferred Oct. 15 on Wake Island); he told a reporter that it was a pity that columnists and reporters for a certain press association could not understand the ideas of two intellectually honest men when they met; he said that MacArthur was loyal to the President and his foreign policy, that he wished a lot of newspapers were, and that there was no disagreement between him and MacArthur (he had just ordered suppressed MacArthur's statement to the Veterans of Foreign Wars, which got into print anyway); this was called "one of his angriest outbreaks in public."

October 26, 1950—He told a Dutch correspondent that the U.S. did not expect war in Europe this winter; he said that he had received a report from fifteen European statesmen that Russia did not want a war then; he wondered where Harold Stassen got his information that after the election the administration planned to recognize the Chinese Communist regime and urge its seating in the U.N.; he said that so far as the U.S. knew there had been only one atomic explosion in Russia; he said that he might call a post-election special session of Congress and might soon make campaign speeches himself.

November 2, 1950—He said that it would be a long time before Spain got an ambassador from the U.S. and that the reporters would have plenty of time to think it over (on December 27, he nominated Stanton Griffis to be ambassador to Spain); he volunteered a ringing indorsement of Helen Gahagan Douglas, Democratic candidate for Senator from California, but failed to mention the candidacy of James Roosevelt, Democrat, for governor of California.

November 16, 1950—In a formal statement read at his news conference, he told Red China that the U.S. planned no invasion of Chinese territory and urged China not to be deceived by Russia as to U.S. intentions; he said that if the Communists wanted peace "they will not take upon themselves the responsibility for obstructing the objectives of the U.N. in Korea"; he pledged the U.S. to adhere to the U.N. plan to localize the conflict in Korea; he again said that Acheson would remain as Secretary of State—the outcome of the election made no difference; he insisted that he was not blue over Republican gains and would continue to press for the entire Fair Deal program; he added that the time was not ripe for pay and price ceilings and refused comment on his plans for 1952 despite predictions that he would run.

November 30, 1950—He declared that the U.S. was fighting for "national security and survival" and that, reluctantly, it would use the atom bomb and all other available weapons if they were needed in any showdown; his words stirred worldwide speculation that the bomb might be used soon against the Korean and Chinese Communists; three hours later a formal White House statement set this speculation at rest by emphasizing that he had not authorized its employment; the later statement warned against "misrepresentation," but said that the use of the bomb had been considered since the outbreak of the Korean war; the disclosure resulted in guarded and apprehensive comment in Europe and sensational headlines here; at the news conference, he once more defended Acheson and MacArthur with a diatribe against the press for spreading lies about people in government, and said that he was "going to bust loose on the reporters some one of these days"; he denied that MacArthur had exceeded his authority in sending troops beyond where they were supposed to go in Korea; he also announced the appointment of DiSalle as director of price stabilization, and later that Prime Minister Attlee was coming to Washington to discuss the world crisis.

December 19, 1950—He named Gen. Eisenhower supreme allied commander in Europe and announced that U.S. forces would be sent to Europe as quickly as they could be assembled and shipped, but for security reasons he refused to say how many; he again insisted that Acheson would remain.

January 4, 1951—He said that all price and wage controls permitted by law would be applied as soon as possible; he stated that eventually there would be a complete across-the-board control of prices and wages; he also said that this country probably would not bomb Communist China without a formal declaration of war by Congress and there was no present intention of making such an attack; in any case it would not attack without U.N. authority and it was not seeking such authority; he again said that the U.S. was not formally at war but was carrying out an obligation of the U.N.; he would not comment on prospects of staying out of war in 1951, but hoped that the U.S. would not get involved; "At what point would you have to consult Congress on the constitutional right to declare war?" he was asked; he replied he would take care of that when the time came; he repeated that the U.S. was always willing to negotiate and that he did not have to ask Congressional approval to send troops to Europe.

January 11, 1951—He said that he would consult Congress as to sending troops to Europe but made it clear that he would not ask Congressional permission to do so; as Commander-in-Chief he insisted that he did not have to do so and he accepted "with vigor" the challenge of those in Congress who would seek to exercise control over such troop movements by tying up military appropriations; he denied any intention of abandoning any part of the Fair Deal program, but seemed resigned to keeping the Taft-Hartley Act; he again made it clear that the U.S. would send more troops to Western Europe under Eisenhower's command.

January 18, 1951—He astonished reporters by declaring not a single U.S. newspaper had printed his statment, made at the January 11 news conference, that he was ready to consult with Congressional committees before sending American troops to Europe. He also complained that his remarks of November 30 about the atom bomb were badly garbled and that this created an entirely unnecessary argument; (a quick check of leading newspapers and the major press associations showed that *all* of them had reported his readiness to consult Congress on sendng additional troops to Europe); he said that he would also appreciate it most highly in this emergency if reporters would state the facts as he stated them; he said that the U.S. would exert every pressure to persuade the U.N. to condemn Communist China as an aggressor following its rejection of the U.N. cease-fire offer.

January 25, 1951—He announced that he was throwing the full weight of his office, Congress and the American people behind the U.S. resolution in the U.N. condemning Communist China as an aggressor in Korea and read a strongly worded statement backing the U.S. demand; he said he was unable to understand the reluctance of Britain, Canada and the Arab-Asian nations to go along; "For my part, I believe in calling an aggressor an aggressor," he said.

February 8, 1951—He branded as "asinine" the report of the Senate Banking subcommittee accusing R.F.C. directors of yielding to political pressure and influence emanating in part from the White House; he denounced the subcommittee and its chairman, Sen. Fulbright; he insisted that he could find no fault with any of the loans and no basis for the charges involving Donald Dawson and Wm. P. Boyle, Jr.; he said that he planned an R.F.C. reorganization scheme; an order to the striking railroad workers to return to work by 4 p.m. February 10 was read at the conference; the President accused the Brotherhood chiefs of breaking their promises like Russia, a statement which "shocked" labor leaders and led to a later White House statement that he did not mean "the rank and file of these unions"; he also dared Congress to cut his 71½ billion dollar budget, a challenge promptly taken up by the Republicans and by the more economy-minded Democrats.

February 15, 1951—He said that the question of U.N. forces in Korea crossing the 38th Parallel was a strategic matter for Gen. MacArthur to decide; the statement was in conflict with the declared policy of the British government (in a statement February 12 by Prime Minister Attlee) and seemed in conflict with a State Department statement which said it was consulting with other governments on the question; in a later statement the White House said that it had not intended to contradict the Acheson statement.

March 15, 1951—(at Key West)—He defended his administration as made up of honorable people and said he hoped that it would be remembered for its efforts to win world peace and help the backward peoples of the world; asked about newspaper criticism of the moral and ethical standards of some White House employees, he replied, "It isn't true, it just isn't true"; he hoped that the next six years would not be as hard as the first six years of his Presidency, but laughingly admonished reporters not to draw conclusions as to whether he would seek re-election in 1952; "All a President of the United States can do," he said, "is to endeavor to make the government—the executive branch—run in the public interest. I have striven very hard to accomplish that purpose"; he contended that no President's administration could be correctly evaluated during his term; *re* a demand by Sen. Knowland that he return to Washington and clean house, he insisted that his house was always clean; he again said that the question of U.N. forces crossing the 38th Parallel was up to Gen. MacArthur and said that he could not comment on the prospects for peace in Korea; he repeated that there had been no change in the U.S. policy of striving in U.N. for specific proposals on disarmament and control of atomic energy since 1945.

From even this partial calendar of the Truman news conferences for the period indicated, the advantages and disadvantages of the conference as a channel of communication between the chief executive and the American public, or between the President and the world, are fairly apparent. The advantages may be summarized as follows:

1. The conference affords a fairly direct way for the President to announce executive action or policy, and to explain his viewpoint on issues.
2. It makes possible, for domestic or world-wide consumption, a democratic exchange between the chief executive and the press and radio correspondents on matters of interest and importance to the public.
3. It multiplies the possibilities of the White House as a sounding board for making, shaping and alerting public opinion.
4. In its limited way, subject always to the willingness of the President to respond, it is an American equivalent of the British device for questioning the government on matters of policy.
5. However it may vary from time to time or from administration to administration, its cumulative effect is to make the executive more responsible and more responsive to the public.

Similarly, the disadvantages may be defined as follows:

1. Such news conferences are always subject to the pleasure and convenience of the incumbent President, and he is not absolutely bound either to continue them or to submit to them on the same basis as formerly.
2. Since this is the case, they are somewhat irregular and lack uniformity.
3. They are often ineffective since the President may, as Franklin

D. Roosevelt and Mr. Truman have frequently done, turn off a leading question with a curt and final "No comment!", from which there is no appeal.

4. Although recent practice has been for the White House secretariat to rehearse the President on the probable questions at the next news conference, its impromptu nature lays the President open to being caught off guard with what could be serious consequences.

5. While the correspondents, who police their own membership, are of high caliber, the President is always at the mercy of the least among them, and this danger is heightened somewhat by the rule that the President may not be quoted directly except by express permission.

Doubtless other advantages and disadvantages might be cited, but the principal ones are those given. Weighing the one group against the other, the scales are still strongly tipped in favor of the presidential news conferences.

Much depends, of course, upon the President himself as to whether the conferences are fruitful. For the most part he lays down the rules and makes the conditions under which they are held. If he is cooperative, and not too thin-skinned, they can be very helpful and profitable to the executive, to the press and radio, and, most importantly, to the public. But if the President is arbitrary, if he is unwilling or reluctant to cooperate, or extremely sensitive to press and radio criticism, then the news conferences suffer accordingly. On occasion, as when Mr. Truman has obviously been angry, they lessen the dignity of the President himself, but these are the exceptions rather than the rule.

As far as anyone can tell, the White House news conference is here to stay. After nearly four decades of continuous and expanding use, it appears to be a fixture in the relations between the chief executive and the American people through the media of the press and the radio. It seems doubtful that any future President will find it possible or politic to hamstring it or to do away with it. Even in a time of national emergency it might be more than ever in the public interest to continue such conferences.

One change, however, would add enormously to the effectiveness of the White House news conference. This would be to televise it. To do so would greatly multiply its possibilities for bringing the President, his ideas, his opinions and his actions directly home to millions of Americans. This would not seriously impair the subsequent press and radio reports of such conferences and, if anything, it would serve to

make both the President and his questioners more responsible in their
conduct of them. To televise the regular White House conferences
would greatly enhance the personal touch and would literally bring
them home to the public. Even when the President is away from Washington, as at Key West or elsewhere, such televising would normally
be possible, and it would make still more democratic a major communications device that is uniquely American.

III

TRUMAN: FIRST PHASE

It was a very humble Harry S. Truman who suddenly, although not entirely unexpectedly, found himself President of the United States in the early evening of April 12, 1945. Humility, indeed, best described the former senator from Missouri who, after three brief months as vice-president, in the twinkling of an eye succeeded Franklin D. Roosevelt.

But time and the responsibilities of office work changes in a man and Harry S. Truman has been no exception. It would be inaccurate to say that his first six years in the White House made a new man of him, but the events of the years from 1945 to 1951 clearly made a different man of him. The early doubts and unsureness were replaced by confidence and self-assurance. But if the good will he took with him into his new office yielded inevitably to sharp partisan differences, the growth of his belief in himself and his stubborn, aggressive defense of the men and the measures to which he gave his approval were no less marked.

When he became President, Mr. Truman announced that for the most part he would continue the Roosevelt policies. Among these were the White House news conferences although, as will be seen, he soon made certain changes in them and conducted them somewhat differently. One of his first steps was to persuade Charles G. Ross, a close personal friend of many years and one of the best of the Washington correspondents, to become Presidential press secretary. In the main this appointment was well received.

Mr. Truman retained the Roosevelt rules as to direct quotation and ascription, but instead of the custom of two stated news conferences a week, he scheduled only one—and then only if, in his judgment, it was worth holding. How this worked out may be judged from the fact that in his first six years as President he held 256 such news conferences, or about five every six weeks. By contrast, Mr. Roosevelt in his 147 months in office held 998 such conferences, or better than nine every six weeks. In its way the latter performance was the more remarkable since most of it occurred in a time of global war and during those long years Mr. Roosevelt was often absent from the White House or out of the country. One other change, made in April 1950, was to transfer the scene of the news conferences from the White House to a fourth-floor conference room in the old State, War and Navy building across the street. Correspondents, now seated, also had to identify themselves upon rising to pose a question to Mr. Truman.

At the outset, Mr. Truman's news conferences were generally far shorter than those of his predecessor. Sometimes they were over in 10 or 12 minutes. In the beginning, too, Mr. Truman was given more to short answers than Mr. Roosevelt, and there were times when these quick answers made trouble. But he learned in time and for the most part managed to contain his temper in his dealings with the newsmen.

It was to his credit that in a number of special instances, as at Potsdam and in connection with setting up the United Nations organization, President Truman threw his weight on the side of a free press and a free exchange of world information and opinion. But as in other directions, thanks to obstructionist forces elsewhere in the world, most of these efforts came to nought. The most important fact remains that the President himself was quite sympathetic with the idea of a free press as it is understood and practiced in the English-speaking world.

Mr. Truman held his first news conference April 17, 1945, five days after he took office. It drew a record attendance of 348 correspondents, a testimonial in its way to his popularity at the time. It lasted only 20 minutes but in that time he indicated the rules that would govern material from his news conferences, made routine announcements, and disposed of the questions put to him. *Editor & Publisher* was authority for saying that he began his Presidency with "a larger acquaintance among newspaper men than Hoover or Coolidge ever enjoyed or than Roosevelt had" in 1933.[1]

In Mr. Truman's first year and a half in the White House, the press on the whole treated him rather well. Opposition newspapers were naturally critical of him but at this stage there was none of the personal feuding that marked the Roosevelt period. This was to come later, especially during the campaign of 1948 and after the President made the decision involving the United States in the "police action" in Korea.

Yet even in those first months there were a number of occurrences which cast shadows on the President's relations with the press. He had an occasional tendency to be short and tart with the correspondents. In the summer of 1946, for example, after a vacation trip to sea, Mr.

Truman met the press at Quonset Point, R. I. It was noted that Senator Theodore F. Green, of Rhode Island, was not among those scheduled to call upon him. When asked whether this had any significance, the President said rather warmly that no one had been "invited," that Senator Green was one of his best friends, and warned the correspondents not to try to make a "mess" of that.

Before that time Mr. Truman was reported to have disclosed at an off-the-record news conference that he had summoned Representative Harold Knutson, Republican, of Minnesota, to the White House and that the latter, a member of the House Ways and Means Committee, admitted that he did "not know how to balance the budget and cut taxes." Representative Knutson denied having been at the White House or having talked with Mr. Truman since he became President and called upon him to "kindly correct the misinformation you gave the press." On September 5, 1945 Mr. Truman admitted that he had been mistaken and commented that even Presidents make mistakes. By itself this was relatively unimportant, but it was only one of a number of times corrections or "clarifications" were necessary after a Truman news conference.

Probably the most painful and costly incident in Mr. Truman's early public relations after he entered the White House was his inept handling of the Wallace-Byrnes issue in which two important members of his cabinet were at odds on U.S. foreign policy at a critical moment. It was generally agreed that Henry Wallace was entitled to his personal opinions, but for him as Secretary of Commerce to take a strong stand at variance with administration policy was quite different. Why Mr. Truman did not see the obviousness of this at once was a mystery. Fortunately Byrnes kept quiet for the time being and the President presently resolved the issue by asking for and getting Wallace's resignation.

Washington reporters played one of the chief roles in bringing to light important aspects of this controversy, notably Wallace's earlier and, until then, secret 4,000-word letter to the President on foreign policy and the latter's prior endorsement of Wallace's Madison Square Garden address in which the secretary opposed the Truman-Byrnes policy at Paris. At a news conference the President confirmed the fact that he had approved the Wallace speech in advance but, when public opinion boiled over, Mr. Truman at a special news conference very lamely, to put it gently, tried to explain that his indorsement was only of Wallace's right to express his opinions and not of the secretary's specific views. For the moment, Wallace was permitted to remain in the cabinet on condition that he would keep silent on foreign policy until after the close of the Paris conference, but two days later his resignation was announced at the White House without warning or explanation. *Time* magazine boldly labeled the President's "explanation" of his indorsement of the Wallace speech as "the lie."

Although the shooting war was over in both the European and Pacific theaters within a few months after Mr. Truman took office, Washington correspondents were restive over the continuance of restrictions on what they regarded as legitimate news. The State Department and the White House were the chief targets for these complaints, but a War Department "administrative order" whose effect was to withhold news of troops locations and movements helped to aggravate the situation. The State Department Correspondents' Association made formal protest that its members were being "scooped" by foreign newspapers on diplomatic matters occurring in Washington.

Similarly, at least one written complaint was reported early in 1946 as having been made to Edward T. Folliard, Washington *Post*, then president of the White House Correspondents' Association. The gist of it was that responsible officials at the Executive Office were not available for comment as much as they should have been. Secretary Ross held a daily press conference at which he issued any formal announcements available, answered routine questions, and accepted inquiries for later submission to Mr. Truman. At other times Eben Ayers, assistant to Ross, provided the usual contact. But the correspondents complained that too often a question had to be submitted to whatever woman secretary answered the telephone. The protest to Folliard pointed out:[2]

"If Ross and Ayers are not available or do not get the question straight, the only alternative is to throw a question at the President. Often this involves taking time of the press conference for matters of limited interest. To this extent anyway, the Association is concerned.

"During casual conversations in the last couple of weeks, I have discovered at least two colleagues who have received a run-around and have been understandably exasperated at prolonged delays in getting answers to questions or getting only partial replies to improperly repeated queries. As one of our colleagues put it, 'if the White House press secretaries are to be only propaganda ministers, we ought to know about it'."

Under present-day conditions a capable press secretary is indispensable to the President. For the most part, Mr. Truman was very fortunate in this respect. When he first took office, he asked

Steve Early, who then was serving as appointment secretary, to resume his former position in which he had served Mr. Roosevelt so well. Early did so for several weeks.

In May 1945 Charles G. Ross—schoolmate and longtime friend of President and Mrs. Truman, formerly chief Washington correspondent of the St. Louis *Post-Dispatch,* for some years editor of its editorial page, and a Pulitzer prize winner in 1931—was sworn in as Presidential press secretary. He served notably for five and a half years in that capacity and his sudden death at his White House desk December 5, 1950 was a great loss to Mr. Truman both officially and personally. As a United Press story of the time pointed out, Ross was not only the "go-between for the press and the radio and the President of the United States," but was "a close adviser to the President as well as a friend and counselor. . ." [3]

Mr. Truman paid him high tribute. He commented that Ross "fell at his post a casualty of his fidelity to duty and his determination that our people should know the truth and all the truth in these critical times. More and more all of us came to depend on the counsel on questions of high public policy which he could give out of the wealth of his learning, his wisdom and his far-flung experience." [4] Ross ranked with Early and McIntyre, of the Roosevelt regime, as the best of the Presidential press secretaries.

Upon the death of Ross, Mr. Truman once more drafted Early to fill the post temporarily. But two days later the President named Joseph H. Short Jr., White House correspondent for the Baltimore *Sun,* to this important place. Short became aquainted with Mr. Truman while covering his 1944 campaign for the vice-presidency and when Mr. Truman became President, Short was transferred to the White House beat and continued there until his appointment. It was the first time any President had named an active White House correspondent to the press secretaryship. Short had served variously with newspapers in the South, the Associated Press in Washington, and the Chicago *Sun* before joining the Baltimore *Sun* in 1943. [5]

While Ross was enormously useful to President Truman in the role of press secretary, his administration of that office did not meet all the needs of the correspondents. He was well liked by most of the correspondents and greatly respected for his own accomplishments, but his office left something to be desired. This was expressed by the White House correspondent of a leading metropolitan daily as follows: [6]

"The most significant thing about Mr. Truman's press relations currently is that they are *efficiently* organized. When Joseph Short suc-

ceeded Charles G. Ross, the most important steps he took were to
add Roger Tubby (from the State Department) and Irving Perlmeter
(from the Internal Revenue Bureau) to the White House press room.
Both of these men are competent, both are anxious to help. They
amount, in fact, to three press secretaries because each is capable
of sitting in a closed meeting and relaying a portion of it to the press.
You can get prompt answers to questions, etc.

"Another important fact is that relations now are friendly between
the reporters assigned to the beat and the Office of the Press Secretary.
All of us were very fond of Charlie Ross as an individual, few of us
thought he personally did a good job as Press Secretary. All of us were
agreed that his office did a very bad job, and that relations were unfriendly between his staff and the newsmen. The symbol of Ross'
administration was a velvet cord strung by his secretary across the
door to the Press Secretary's office to keep reporters *out*. The velvet
cord disappeared as soon as Mr. Short took over.

"Yet it would be wrong to think that relations are perfect. The reporters at the White House frequently complain because Short would
rather say 'no comment' than ask Mr. Truman for a straight answer; yet, in fairness, if you press hard enough, Short will go ask the
President for clarification if you can convince him the query should be
answered.

"Most of those regularly assigned at the White House also feel that
Short, on more than one occasion, has tried to come between the reporter and other White House staff members—that they are, in brief,
urged not to talk to reporters lest news be given out without clearance
by Mr. Short. It isn't too hard, however, to get around this if one
is willing to keep trying."

Cameramen have enjoyed a somewhat better status under the Truman regime than under that of his predecessor. "Mostly they are
resigned to the restrictions and the system and the protocol," James
L. Collings reported in *Editor & Publisher*, "and they find compensa-
tion in the many good features of covering the White House." Milton
Freier, of Acme, testified of Mr. Truman that "Of all the guys I've
ever photographed, he's the most human I've met." Ross declared
"There are very friendly relations between the photographers and
President Tuman . . . He frequently calls them by their first names
and jokes with them." Mr. Truman dubbed the White House photo-
raphers "The One More Club" and they showed their regard for him by
giving him a still camera and a movie camera in 1947.[7] But like Pres-

ident Franklin Roosevelt, Mr. Truman did not care to be photographed while eating.

Over the years Mr. Truman addressed newspaper groups such as
the American Society of Newspaper Editors on several occasions, both
on and off the record. One of these occasions was the annual meeting
of the Associated Press in 1947. By tradition only one toast is proposed at such conventions. This is to the health of the President of
the United States. That year for the first time since 1929 the Chief
Executive was there in person to acknowledge the toast, when he
spoke April 21 at the A. P. luncheon meeting. One of the best of
these talks, described as "the best he ever made in his life," was an
off-the-record speech to an A.S.N.E. meeting at the A. P. convention.
Mr. Truman began with a tribute to the performance of the U.S.
press in its coverage of the war and administration foreign policy. The
only applause to interrupt his address came when he described these as
"examples of the finest effort of a free, responsible press"—with emphasis on the last three words. In his address, the President made
these direct references to the press:[8]

"Freedom, in the American tradition, is always coupled with service. The American press—a free press—must never forget its obligation to the American people. Its treatment of the recent war and its
discussion of our present foreign policy are examples of the finest effort of a free, responsible press. Without abandoning constructive
criticism, the press, with rare exceptions, has carried the facts fully
and fairly to the American people, so that they could be the judge.

"We are now at a stage in our national economic life when the American press can render similar service. The manner in which the American press makes clear to our citizens the problems that we face in
maintaining our prosperity—and the reasons why it is essential to advance that prosperity—can help determine the future welfare of every
family in the United States . . .

"The men and women here today, and the rest of the press of the
nation, have a great opportunity for service at this time. Not only
must the facts be presented, but there must be brought home to our
people the seriousness of the issue and the need for united effort for
the good of all, rather than separate effort for the benefit of any single
group.

"I take comfort in the knowledge that the press of this country will
accept this opportunity for service in the same high spirit with which
it has always served this nation."

However cordially the assembled publishers welcomed the President, the same cordiality did not extend to the news and editorial columns of some of their newspapers. One was the New York *Daily News* which took editorial note of his references to the press, especially as to how the newspapers, in its paraphrase, could tell "the people how we can promote and increase prosperity and defeat inflation." It went on: "It then appeared that the press could do this noble work by bally-hooing the Truman economic ideas. Of course, newspapers which favor Mr. Truman will peddle these ideas, while anti-New Deal papers will try to tear a few holes in them." The *Daily News* then proceeded to do the latter. The New York *Sun* went farther. In advance of his address, the President was greeted by a Page One editorial in the *Sun's* night edition with the caption, "YOU, Mr. Truman, You Made Prices What They Are Today." Set in 2-column, 10-point over four columns, the editorial held that position all through the day despite changes in the banner headlines before, during and after Mr. Truman's visit.[9]

The election of 1948 was a tremendous turning point in the public career of Harry S. Truman. Not only did it make him President in his own right for a full four-year term, but it gave him a degree of self-confidence that amounted to cocksureness and approached the aplomb of Franklin D. Roosevelt himself. In addition, it once more put the bulk of the newspapers of the country on the losing side of a Presidential campaign.

Almost no one of any public or political importance except himself believed Mr. Truman would win. But he kept insisting that he would be elected. He derided the public opinion polls—which, with one or two exceptions, forecast Dewey's election—as being inaccurate and as unreliable reflections of public opinion. But if the polls and the press were mistaken in their judgments of the moment, they had plenty of company. Even the professional politicians were nearly unanimous in their belief that Mr. Truman could not win. In the end, the President's margin of victory in terms of the electoral college was decisive, 303 to 189, but on the basis of the popular vote it was much less pronounced, 24,105,812 to 21,970,065. In any case, it was a *personal* rather than a party victory.

In a preliminary poll, *Editor & Publisher* reported in its September 11, 1948 issue that Governor Dewey led President Truman "four to one in the volume of newspaper support given by the nation's dailies." Specifically, it said the Republican candidate had support "from 68.68 per cent of the dailies[10] comprising 70.4 per cent of the daily circulation. Truman trails with backing from 16.16 per cent of the papers[11] accounting for 13.99 per cent of the circulation." The remaining 4.15 percent accounted for were divided between Thurmond, the Dixiecrat candidate, and Henry Wallace, neither of whom had any appreciable newspaper support. The remaining 10.91 percent of the dailies[12] were "independent or undecided." [13]

Three days before the election *Editor & Publisher* made a final report on this situation. It included 1,183 dailies as against only 723 in the earlier survey. It also showed that daily newspaper support of Dewey was still running four to one over Truman, but in terms of circulation the ratio had risen from five to one early in September to eight to one late in October. The support for Thurmond and Wallace was still negligible, but 15.38 percent of the dailies remained "independent." Even in his home state of Missouri, President Truman had the support of only 13 dailies to Dewey's 14, with combined circulations of but 44,569 to 1,326,397, respectively.[14]

Inevitably there was editorial soul-searching in the wake of the election. "Again, as in '36, '40, and '44," *Editor & Publisher* commented, "the Democratic Presidential candidate won the election in the face of majority newspaper support for his Republican rival. Once again, the skeptics, critics and even the 'man in the street' are mumbling 'the newspapers don't reflect the interests of their readers,' and 'you can't believe what you read in the newspapers.'" In rebuttal it pointed out the absence of a "national press" in the United States and cited the further fact that "28 states voted in line with the majority newspaper support for the candidates." As of the night after the election, it added, Mr. Truman had "won his battle with the electoral votes of 28 states in which he was victorious." It went on: "So, in more than 50 per cent of the states a majority of the newspapers either rode the right horse or were influential in bringing home a winner. But, as yet, no one has commended the newspapers for this voting record as good as Truman's." "Actually," it concluded, "the daily newspapers deserve tribute for the fair, complete and unbiased presentation of the election issues enabling the electorate to make its choice." [15]

But others were more introspective. James B. Reston, Pulitzer prize-winning reporter of the New York *Times,* in a letter to the editor of that newspaper declared: "Before we in the newspaper business spend all our time and energy analyzing Governor Dewey's failure in the election, maybe we ought to try to analyze our own failure. For that failure is almost as spectacular as the President's victory, and the quicker we admit it the better off we'll be."

Reston found a number of reasons to explain the results. One was the failure of "almost every political reporter" to take account of the fact "that a defeated candidate had never been nominated and elected after his defeat" and that "the national income was running at a rate of $210 billion dollars a year, that over 61,000,000 persons were employed at unprecedentedly high wages, and that the people had seldom if ever turned against the Administration in power at such a time." In brief, according to Reston "we overestimated the tangibles and underestimated the intangibles; we relied too much on techniques of reporting." The great intangible of the election, he concluded "was the political influence of the Roosevelt era on the thinking of the nation. It was less dramatic than the antics of Messrs. Wallace and Thurmond, but in the long run it was more important and we didn't give enough weight to it. Consequently we were wrong, not only on the election, but, what's worse, on the whole political direction of our time." [16]

The Washington *Post*, in a telegram to President Truman who was still at Independence, Mo., the day after election, invited him "to attend a 'crow banquet' to which this newspaper proposes to invite newspaper editorial writers, political reporters and editors, including our own, along with pollsters, radio commentators and columnists, for the purpose of providing a repast appropriate to the appetite created by the late election." For Mr. Truman there was to be turkey and white tie, for the others crow and sack cloth. The *Post* hoped that the President would "consent to deliver the address of the evening. As the dean of American election forecasters (and the only accurate one) it is much desired that you share with your colleagues the secret of your analytical success." [17]

In recent years, Mr. Truman has used his news conferences to make a number of announcements of disclosures of worldwide importance. One of these was at his conference of September 23, 1949 to the effect that Russia had produced an atomic explosion. Another was the prepared statement he read at his January 5, 1950 news conference in which, without prior consultation with Congress, he announced a hands-off policy as to Formosa. Republicans in Congress promptly charged him with scuttling the bipartisan foreign policy. At his press meeting of June 1, 1950, twenty-four days before South Korea was invaded, he declared that the world was closer to a really permanent peace than it had been in five years. Similarly, at his August 31, 1950 session with the newsmen he again gave Defense Secretary Johnson his full backing and denied that he was considering any change in that secretaryship. Twelve days later Johnson resigned.

In a formal statement read at his November 16, 1950 news conence, he notified Red China—and the world—that the United States planned no invasion of Chinese territory and urged China not to be deceived by Russia as to American intentions. Two weeks later he caused momentary world-wide jitters by his statement that, reluctantly, the United States would use the atom bomb and all other available weapons if they were needed in any showdown. This led to widespread speculation as to whether the bomb might be used soon against the North Korean and Chinese Communists. There were political repercussions from his statement at his January 11, 1951 news conference that he would consult Congress as to sending troops to Europe but insisted he did not have to ask its permission to do so. On February 8, 1951 he set off more political fireworks when he labeled as "asinine" the report of the Senate banking sub-committee accusing the Reconstruction Finance Corporation directors of yielding to political pressure and influence coming in part from the White House.

On a number of occasions Mr. Truman showed anger or other signs of temper at his news conferences. At the February 9, 1950 session, he replied to a columnist's question with, "You needn't put any words in my mouth." When the correspondents rather objected to an exclusive interview Mr. Truman granted early in 1950 to Arthur Krock, of the New York *Times*, as contrary to custom, the President made it plain at his news conference the next day that the custom would continue but he was not bound by it, that he was "his own free agent" and would "see whom he pleased and say what he pleased and he was not to be censured by them or anybody else." He added that he did not like their attitude and "they ought to cool off!" [18] Four days after he had met with General MacArthur on Wake Island in October 1950 he exploded at the question whether he and MacArthur were in complete agreement on Formosa. He insisted that the general was loyal to the President and his foreign policy and he wished a lot of newspapers were.

At his November 16, 1950 news conference, the one at which he spoke of the possible use of the atom bomb—promptly "clarified" by a White House statement several hours later—he again defended Secretary Acheson and General MacArthur. In anger, he declared that he was "going to bust loose on the reporters some one of these days." At his January 18, 1951 meeting with the newsmen he astonished them by asserting that not a single U. S. newspaper printed his statement at the January 11 news conference that he was ready to consult with Congressional committees before sending U. S. troops to Europe. (A check showed that all of the press associations and leading newspapers had carried his earlier statement accurately.)   Such outbursts did not help his relations with the correspondents.   Fuel was added to this fire by such impulsive acts by Mr. Truman as his angry letter to Paul Hume, music critic of the Washington *Post,* for what Mr. Truman called a "lousy review" of Margaret Truman's concert of December 5, 1950 in Washington.   The President wrote Hume he sounded "like a frustrated old man who never made a success" and intimated that if he ever met the critic the latter would "need a new nose and plenty of beefsteak." [19]

But nothing Mr. Truman said or did aroused the newspapers as much as his order of September 25, 1951 extending to all government agencies handling military information the tight security already in force in the State and Defense Departments.   While the President insisted that the order was designed against "disclosure harmful to the security of the United States," there were immediate and widespread protests.   The order applied to government officials and employes only, but the press and radio feared that it might lead to unreasonable suppression of legitimate news.

Their fears were heightened when the Office of Price Stabilization that same day issued a staff memorandum to withhold from the pubilc any information which might embarrass OPS.   Word of this move leaked out two days later.   President Truman immediately ordered the directive withdrawn lest it "might be construed" as an outgrowth of his own order.   He also tried to allay the fears of the correspondents at his weekly news conference.   But he not only defended the order and insisted he would let it stand until it was proved harmful, but charged that U. S. newspapers and magazines had already published 95 percent of this country's security information.   This accusation angered the press further since much of the information had been released by the military.

Alexander F. Jones, of the Syracuse *Herald-Journal,* president of the American Society of Newspaper Editors, spoke out against the order.   James S. Pope, of the Louisville *Courier-Journal,* chairman of the ASNE committee on freedom of information, called it "ill-advised and poorly executed."   There were protests in both houses of Congress, as well as by the Associated Press Managing Editors Association, in convention, and by many individual newspapers and commentators.

On the basis of the record, five or six conclusions seem evident as to Mr. Truman's press relations after six years.

1. It is to his credit that he has continued to hold stated news con-

ferences with few interruptions; this is important not only to the press
and the radio but to the public.

2. Making allowance for all the personal and other factors involved,
he has acquitted himself rather creditably in his news conferences although not as well as Mr. Roosevelt did.

3. On occasion, however, important "slips" have occurred resulting
in embarrassment to the President personally or to the administration
or to others; with more adroit handling, most of these could have been
prevented.

4. Despite his recent objection to the term and his insistence that
his attitude is only one of confidence, it is generally agreed that the
President has had a marked air of cocksureness since the 1948 election.

5. There are also some veteran Washington observers who feel
that, like Mr. Hoover and Mr. Roosevelt toward the end of their tenure, Mr. Truman has had a growing tendency of late toward a persecution complex.

6. Yet in the face of mounting press criticism of his administration,
the correspondents and others generally have a personal liking for Mr.
Truman.

Part of this was summed up by a longtime Washington reporter in
these words:[20]

". . . practically everyone has a personal liking for Mr. Truman. This
applies to newspapermen as well as to everyone else. They disapprove
of him or criticize him with their intellectual faculties, but on the human front they feel warm toward him. I do not know anyone, either
pressman or other, who feels anything except personal warmth for
Truman the man.

"Of course, everyone misses the brilliant repartee of the Roosevelt
conferences. He was on his toes in these sessions, and usually knew
exactly what he was saying. Mr. Truman, by contrast, is a dull man,
and he often says things which the reporters know are not thought
through or are impulsive . . .

"When Mr. Truman was new in office, he was scairt. Being essential-
ly a modest man, he felt overwhelmed by the responsibilities of his office. He reflected this timidity in talks with newspapermen. I think
they all respected him for that attitude, and were inclined to be easy
with him and not make too much of the contrast between him and his
predecessor.

"After the 1948 elections, however, Mr. Truman became obviously
cocky in his dealings with the newsmen, and with practically all others.
Mind you, this isn't arrogance. It's just cockiness. It arises out of

his feeling that he won the election. He did—not his party—he did. This is pretty much true. The reporters recognize the fact, and they don't rough him much on account of his self-assurance . . . .

"Rather recently, it seems to me that I have detected in Mr. Truman the beginnings of a feeling of persecution. Newspaper criticism, for example, he often considers unfair. I think perhaps this grows out of the rise of what I call cockiness. He feels pretty sure of himself, and anyone who criticizes him does so, he thinks, out of evil motives. The interesting thing is that I have seen the same thing in two other Presidents, Roosevelt and Hoover. I think it is an occupational malady which comes upon any man after he has several years of adulation."

Much this same sort of comment was given quite independently by another correspondent who has been dealing with the Washington scene for nearly 20 years. He differed with the writer just quoted as to Truman's popularity. He wrote, in part:[21]

"There has been the normal amount of irritation among reporters covering the White House regularly over 'favoritism' to certain reporters—the Arthur Krock interview which won Pulitzer recognition, the material made available to Jonathan Daniels and John Hersey. Truman . . . made it clear that he'd do as he pleased in that respect, but the grumbling continues.

"In the early days, Truman was more outspoken than he is now. He learned caution by some early sad experiences and 'no comment' now appears more frequently in his vocabulary.

"There have been instances in which Truman has attempted to shift to the reporters the responsibility for his own misstatements. In such instances as his 'clarification' of his statement about the use of the atomic bomb, the implication was that he was inaccurately represented, or emphasis was improperly placed. A more recent case was his statement that he had considered removing MacArthur for a year before the event occurred. He 'clarified' this a day later, but when you read the transcript of that conference, you find that he was given every opportunity to say what he meant; in fact, the question was repeated a couple of times.

"Certainly the instances in which he has been misquoted have been very rare; invariably the difficulties have arisen from misstatements on his part or his failure to make himself clear. The correspondents, of course, always resent the inference of sloppy reporting.

"Truman has been a source of worry to his press secretaries. The late Charley Ross was embarrassed on a number of occasions because Truman did not take him into his confidence. The result was that stories would appear about which Charley knew nothing. A check would reveal them to be factual.

"Steve Early . . . never had that difficulty. From the beginning, he had an understanding with Roosevelt that he was to be advised on all matters which might become news and, so far as I know, Roosevelt never held out on him.

"The present secretary, Joe Short, has tried to avoid the consequences of such embarrassing incidents as Truman's penchant for early-morning letter writing, but I am not sure he has been one hundred per cent successful.

"Truman is far from being as adroit as Roosevelt in the give-and-take of the news conference. Often he gives the appearance of being uneasy; whereas Roosevelt always enjoyed the sparring. He has one cliché which turns up in nearly every conference: 'We will cross that bridge when we come to it.' I've long since lost count of the bridges, crossed and uncrossed.

"Truman does not berate the press as Roosevelt did . . . Truman tosses an occasional harpoon, but doesn't give the lectures we used to hear from F.D.R.

"Truman does not enjoy the admiration among reporters that Roosevelt had . . . Truman . . . is not highly regarded by reporters and columnists who support the principles of his Fair Deal."

The metropolitan correspondent, previously quoted, also commented on Mr. Truman's accessibility for news and interviews. He wrote:

"So far as the President is concerned, he is likely to be much more generous with news, and with making facilities available for obtaining stories, than is his Press Office. One need refer only to the John Hersey series, which was arranged personally with the President and never would have got to first base if it had been left up to the Press Secretary for approval. Reporters who need to know when a safe time might be to take a vacation so as not to miss big Presidential news can get no help from the Press Office; yet, on the same day, Mr. Truman told reporters that *July* would be okay.

"The President himself is much more sure-footed in his dealings with the Press than when he first took office. He knows what questions to dodge, and which to answer. In the early days, one had a feeling he tried very hard to answer every question to help the reporter out—often he didn't know what he was talking about and the result was embarrassment and, not infrequently, exposure of division within the Administration.

"He seems to enjoy his press conferences, especially since the Mac-Arthur incident. And he has used the press to get in some rough counter punches at the General."

In sum, if Mr. Truman's relations with the press have sometimes been stormy and if that relationship has sometimes been less fruit-ful than either the press or the President might desire, the important thing is that he has continued his news conferences with few inter-ruptions. In six years he has submitted to freely asked questions even though he cannot always give the desired answers. It is still significant that of all the capitals of the world Washington is the only one where this democratic process is possible.

To a group of callers at the White House in December 1950 Mr. Truman remarked that he was handicapped by "living the lives of two men" and it was sometimes difficult to keep the human being in subjec-tion. In October 1947 Bert Andrews, chief of the Washington bureau of the New York *Herald Tribune,* wrote: "At the Presidential press conference—one of the best continuing manifestations of the way American democracy works—there were surface indications for saying that Mr. Truman was, by turns, irritable, calm, irascible, humorous, sensitive and thick-skinned. Beneath the surface—and not too far beneath—were the Presidential worries that made some wonder why he wasn't more irritable, irascible and sensitive, and less calm, humor-ous and thick-skinned." This was another way of saying that even a President is human and the burdens of his office are enough to make him more so on occasion. If Mr. Truman's press relations have not always been the best on record they have been better than those of most of his predecessors.

IV

TRUMAN: SECOND PHASE

Although no two Presidents are alike, Harry S. Truman to the end of his term remained "different," often unpredictable, sometimes inconsistent, and occasionally just plain contrary. In his nearly eight years in the White House he learned for the most part to control his temper but there were times when it still betrayed him. On the whole, his relations with the White House correspondents were good but he retained much of his distrust of the press and his belief (a) that it was often unfair to him and his administration and (b) that it did not accurately reflect public opinion.

To the end he continued to meet the correspondents with a fair degree of regularity. Despite their occasional differences this was important from the standpoint of the basic right of the people to know. This was especially true during a time of tension with the "cold war" in full swing, the action in Korea often confused, the actions of the United Nations frequently uncertain, and the future course of events clouded with doubt.

During his 93 months as President, Mr. Truman held a total of 324 news conferences. This was an average of nearly three and a half conferences a month. In his last two years they averaged about two every three weeks. In his 147 months in office, Mr. Roosevelt, by contrast, held 998 such conferences or at the rate of nearly seven a month. But where his predecessor tried to maintain stated press conferences, Mr. Truman's policy was to hold them fairly frequently but only when the circumstances justified them.

A number of events or developments marked Mr. Truman's last two years in the White House with respect to press relations. Among the more important of these were the following:

1. The issuance of his controversial order of September 25, 1951, extending to all government agencies handling military information the tight security in force in the State and Defense Departments.

2. The sudden death of Press Secretary Joseph T. Short in 1952.

3. Mr. Truman's insistent defense of his administration against mounting charges of graft and corruption among Federal agencies and officials.

4. The aggressive part he played in the 1952 campaign, punctuated by "digs" at the press.

5. The implication that he had power in an emergency to seize the press and radio.

6. His unprecedented action in permitting William Hillman, veteran correspondent, to have access to his personal diaries and private papers, with special interviews.

7. His equally unprecedented step in the last weeks of his administration in giving personal interviews to a handful of correspondents.

8. His comments and interviews in the first weeks of his retirement after which he sealed his lips for the most part for an indefinite period.

In June 1951 there were some who saw a change in the Truman manner. Andrew Tully, a Scripps-Howard writer, recalled that some weeks earlier the President told the press he preferred to be described as "confident" rather than "cocky." Tully went on: "Now he seems to be working at the job of proving his point. The President always has been a light-hearted man, quick to josh and appreciative of the phrase that brings grins to men's faces. But almost overnight there is a new sedateness in his manner; he is far more businesslike, far more serious generally in his approach to the press." But there were limits to the change in Mr. Truman. "If anybody was thinking Mr. Truman had softened up," Tully added, "he soon was disenchanted. Asked what he thought of Secretary of State Acheson's appearance at the MacArthur hearings, the President worked in a crack at the opposition. Mr. Acheson, he snapped, was doing fine; he was telling the truth and the truth seldom was told by the opposition." [1]

It was at this same conference on June 7, 1951 that the President excited renewed speculation as to the possibility of his seeking another term. This came in answer to a question concerning the suggestion of Senator Paul H. Douglas of Illinois that if Mr. Truman did not choose to run, both major parties might nominate General Eisenhower. The Truman retort was in the form of a question: "With Senator Douglas as Vice President?" [2] Mr. Truman was more loquacious at some news conferences than others. At his June 21 conference, by contrast, he and the correspondents had a quiet time chiefly because he dodged controversial questions.

The specter of the 1952 campaign kept cropping up in White House news conferences a year before the national conventions met. On July 19, 1951 Mr. Truman told the correspondents he was as mystified as anyone as to whether General Eisenhower would be a candidate. In the short space of nine minutes the President replied to questions on ten different topics ranging from Russia's A-bomb experiments to the key to the French Bastille. This was a sample of the quick give-and-take between the correspondents and the Chief Executive, although the speed with which the conferences were conducted was sometimes to his disadvantage.

At his August 2, 1951 news conference the President said in reply to a question that he did not believe General Eisenhower's duties in Europe would interfere if the general was in a political frame of mind in 1952.[3] A week later he "nominated" Senator Robert A. Taft for President on the Republican ticket, voiced the opinion that General Eisenhower was not a candidate for the Democratic nomination, but was coy as ever as to his own plans.[4]

By all odds the most controversial step by Mr. Truman affecting the press in 1951, and one of the most criticized actions he ever took, was his order of September 25, 1951 extending a system of government restrictions designed to deny information of military value to potential enemies. The President specifically disclaimed any intention of keeping legitimate news from the public and insisted that the sole intent was to guard against disclosures "harmful to the security of the United States." The order extended to all government agencies handling military information the same tight security previously in effect in the State and Defense Departments. It applied only to officials and to government employes and made no effort to limit what could be published by newspapers or broadcast by radio stations. Under the order thereafter certain material had to be classified as "security information"—top secret, secret, confidential, or restricted.

There were immediate protests. The newspaper viewpoint was expressed by Alexander F. Jones, of Syracuse, president of the American Society of Newspaper Editors. "Any time you give a government department head authority to classify material as top secret on a security basis," he contended, "you are placing a potent weapon in his hands. The result, invariably, is further suppression of the news." A similar attitude was voiced by James S. Pope, of Louisville, chairman of the ASNE committee on freedom of information. He called the order "ill advised and poorly executed," expressing the fear that the order was more likely to "smother legitimate information about the operation of government."[5]

A development the very next day played directly into the hands of the critics. This was in the form of an Office of Price Stabilization staff memo to withhold any information which might be embarrassing. There was an immediate uproar and exactly 129 minutes after word

of the memo leaked out President Truman personally ordered it re-
scinded, with the explanation that it "might be misconstrued" as an
outgrowth of his own order on security material. There was a minor
mystery as to who wrote the OPS order.[6]

The Truman order stood, meanwhile, in the face of heavy fire. A
New York *Herald Tribune* headline over a Washington story asked
whether it was "Security or Censorship?"[7] The Dayton *Journal
Herald* called it a "Dangerous Curb on News,"[8] and to the Cleveland
Plain Dealer it was "An Evil Order."[9] The Inland Daily Press Association and the Associated Press Managing Editors Association made
formal protests. The latter called the order "a dangerous instrument
of news suppression" which extended the "cloak of military security"
to civilian agencies. Mr. Truman told the AP editors' group "he
would not hesitate to modify the order on the basis of constructive
suggestions as long as the basic safeguards were maintained."[10] Nothing came of this and later the President was critical of the AP group
for not "being at all helpful."

To Raymond Moley, "Truman's assertion that the press will have to
censor security information is a confession that the Federal Administration cannot itself protect its secrets."[11] Robert McLean, of Philadelphia, president of the Associated Press, declared that the Truman
order invited "a creeping censorship of a kind never before established
in this country in time of peace or even in a time of war."

At his October 4 news conference the President blamed "newspapers
and slick magazines" for the issuance of the order. He contended that
"95 percent of our secret information has been published by newspapers and slick magazines." He took the view that it did not matter
who gave out such information and in some cases editors should withhold it even when it was made public by the Defense and other departments. Publishers had no business using it, he declared, if they
had the welfare of the country at heart. But his stand was "clarified"
several hours later by a statement from Press Secretary Short to the
effect that it was safe to publish information put out for publication by
"responsible officials" qualified to judge its relationship to security.

If experience so indicated Mr. Truman was willing to change the
security order but he defended it as a reasonable approach to a difficult
problem. He again insisted he had no desire to curb freedom of the
press and was only trying to keep the country from being wiped out.
He ascribed the statement that "the newspapers and slick magazines"
had published 95 percent of U.S. military secrets to a Yale University
study given to the Central Intelligence Agency.[12]

This exchange touched off another round of argument which settled nothing. In some respects the issue was more confused than ever, especially in view of the "clarification" of the President's own remarks. Columnist Jay Franklin demanded "Whom Does Truman Think He Fools?" [13] David Lawrence declared similarly, "Truman's Charge Against Press Is Stupid and Tragic." [41]

Six weeks later at Key West, Fla., Mr. Truman set off another row over what he called fake cease-fire stories from Korea. At his November 29 news conference there he first read a prepared statement in which he declared that the United Nations would continue to bring pressure on the Communists until an armistice was signed. He then gave the correspondents an off-the-cuff lecture. For example, he recalled the premature World War I armistice story by Roy W. Howard and a current Associated Press story from Seoul to the effect that orders from the highest source, possibly from the White House, had brought ground fighting to a halt in Korea. The President called the Howard story a fake and said the AP story was parallel. He added that he understood the AP story sprang out of the intense competition for news but contended that in such dangerous times the press should be careful to stick to the truth. The welfare of the United Nations and of the United States transcended any competitive situation among newsmen.

There were immediate replies. From New York the Associated Press denied that any competitive "pressure" was in any way involved in its story of the lull in the fighting which remained a mystery. Mr. Truman had been emphatic, moreover, that the date of the Howard story was October 27, 1918 because "it was in his diary." In a statement through the New York *World-Telegram and Sun,* Howard gave the correct date as November 7 and reviewed his explanation of how the false report had been given him in the office of the U.S. admiral commanding at Brest. [15]

In the meantime Secretary Short issued this statement: "After refreshing his memory about his experience of reading a false armistice report in a French newspaper on Oct. 27, 1918, the President is not sure that this report originated with Mr. Roy Howard." [16] Secretary Short, in turn, challenged the accuracy of the AP statement on its story about the alleged cease-fire, contending it was "designed to confuse the American people." To David Lawrence, the Truman "castigation of press associations for their dispatches from Korea on the lull in the fighting there" was "a conspicuous and regrettable example of how officialdom often seeks to blame the press for its own mistakes." [17]

Two weeks later in Washington, in another notable, heavily attended new conference, Mr. Truman defended his administration with the assertion that "wrongdoers have no house with me, no matter who they are or how big they are." At this same conference he denied any plans to remove either Attorney General McGrath or Democratic National Chairman Frank McKinney. He declared firmly that his administration had always acted swiftly to eliminate wrongdoers from its ranks and would continue to do so. This was done also with Communists found working for the government.

Asked for examples of removals, he said that several Cabinet members had been relieved of their posts and the Internal Revenue Collectors in Boston, St. Louis and San Francisco were asked to resign before their alleged shortcomings were brought to light publicly. He asserted that Chairman McKinney suited him "down to the ground," and added that he did not "pull the rug" from under people who please him just because the newspapers don't like them. He indicated that he would take further steps to police the Federal service but it would be on his own initiative at a time of his choosing and that he could not be pushed into doing anything by anyone.[18] He added that it pleased him when the newspapers disliked something he had done because it convinced him he was right.[19] The President was grim and caustic during much of the conference.

When Bert Andrews, of the New York *Herald Tribune,* started to say that one thing that puzzled the reporters, Mr. Truman broke in to say, "You're easily puzzled. You're always speculating about something you don't know anything about. But go ahead." [20] He also singled out the St. Louis *Post-Dispatch* for being guilty of particular bias against Democrats.

One of the most unusual things Mr. Truman ever did was late in his administration to turn over his personal papers and diaries to the correspondent and commentator, William Hillman. This was something no other President had ever done while still in office and almost none after leaving the White House. It went much further than Andrew Johnson had in his defensive interviews between his impeachment and his trial and as far or further than Woodrow Wilson had with Ray Stannard Baker. Specially illustrated, the Hillman volume was published in 1952 by Farrar, Straus and Young under the title of *Mr. President.*[21] Portions of it were widely reprinted at the time, a condensation of it appeared in *Reader's Digest* and it was commented upon extensively.

The book came about because Mr. Truman wanted "the people to know the Presidency as I have experienced it and I want them to know me as I am." To this end the President not only made his personal papers available but supplemented them with interviews which gave Hillman ample opportunity to get additional information. Mr. Truman thought it best to limit the use of material from his diaries to the end of 1949 but this was offset by "direct exposition of his views on major events and his thinking, covering the period from the end of 1949 to date, . . ." [22] The President's willingness to make this material available was of great value in shedding light on his actions, attitudes and policies while he was still in office.

Mr. President was assembled from a variety of materials—formal papers and addresses, rough notes never intended for the light of day, letters to various persons mostly unidentified, miscellaneous papers, and the information supplied in the amplifying interviews. Inevitably there were references to the press, not always commendatory. On a Sunday in October 1951 for example, Mr. Truman wrote an unidentified columnist as follows: [23]

"I've just read your column about my security press conference. You give me credit for the responsibility of the men who were the sources of the information about which I talked. I wish that were true . . . .

"You newspaper men have a complex that anyone who tells you of any of your many shortcomings is either anxious to be a dictator or else he is an ignoramus. But you should take into consideration that we are no longer in the gay nineties of Ben Harrison, William McKinley or Teddy the Rough Rider.

"We are faced with the most terrible responsibility that any nation ever faced . . . if Russia would be a good neighbor and use her military expenditures for her own economic development, I would not have to scold the publishers for giving away our military secrets. Wish you'd do a little soul searching and see if at *great* intervals the President may be right.

"The country is yours as well as mine. You find no trouble in *suppressing* news in which I'm interested. Why can't you do a little safety policing?"

In a memorandum for Senator Connally on September 24, 1945 he noted, "Reported interview this morning in the New York *Times* and the Washington *Post* quotes me as saying that I will assume full responsibility for the policy of the Atomic Bomb. It is not an accurate statement." [24] In his off-the-record remarks on May 11, 1947 at the annual Gridiron Club dinner, he said, in part: "This is the greatest governmental system in the world. Our press has helped to make it so. As I have said before, our press has done a particularly fine job in making clear to the people the full meaning of our policy of aid to Greece and Turkey. Our press can take some share of the credit for the resounding majority which the Greek and Turkish aid bill has just won in the House of Representatives. I am not here just to butter up the press. I do not think it is perfect. But, it is the best press in the world and it's doing a fine job. It is an integral part of our democracy. . . . " [25]

On the basis of newspaper clippings describing him as in bad health, Mr. Truman shortly before Christmas 1947 had fun with a memorandum in which he noted that he ought to read one newspaper's account of his health while keeping his own health certificate before him. Apparently the newspaper in question was the Chicago *Tribune*. The President referred facetiously to various items such as his blood pressure, to recent additions to his Kitchen Cabinet, to the appointments of a Secretary for Inflation, a Secretary of Reaction, a Secretary for Columnists whose duties "are to listen to all radio commentators, read all columnists in the newspapers from ivory tower to lowest gossip, coordinate them and give me the result so I can run the United States and the world as it should be," and a Secretary of Semantics who was to "furnish me 40 to 50 dollar words. Tell me how to say yes and no in the same sentence without a contradiction . . . . He is to show me how to keep silent—and say everything." [26]

Beyond question his election in his own right in 1948 gave Mr. Truman a new measure of self-assurance. Now he was President by the suffrage of the people and not by inheritance. He had confounded the prophets and the pollsters who, almost without exception, could see only defeat for him. Among the undated memoranda of the time were several references to the press. In one he remarked, "Now I have no bitterness in my heart against anyone—not even the bitter opposition press and its henchmen the paid columnists and managing editors and the bought and paid for radio commentators." [27]

From the correspondence Hillman culled a variety of statements reflecting Mr. Truman's attitudes. In one comment to an unidentified correspondent in 1948, the President said, "I have never seen the irritable, petulant and angry President—you probably have been reading certain columnists—they are not really reliable reporters, you

know." [28] In a similar comment in 1950 he said, "I am going to spend
the rest of my life in an endeavor to cause a return to truthful writing
and reporting." [29] And in 1951 he remarked, "Editors are peculiar an-
imals—they throw mud and bricks at you the whole year round—
then they make one favorable statement which happens to agree with
the facts and they think they should be hugged and kissed for it." [30]

Early in 1952 Mr. Truman remained cagey as to his political intentions. At his January 24 news conference he parried all questions as
to his plans except that he would probably announce his intentions before April 29, the deadline in Missouri for filing for U.S. senator. There
had been speculation that he might seek to return to the Senate but
he declined to comment on this.[31] At his January 31 conference he
again refused to indicate his political intentions. This was repeated
on February 14.

Because of his flat refusal to answer certain kinds of questions at
his December 16, 1951 news conference, some correspondents inferred
that an attempt was being made to control the kinds of questions
asked. The New York *Herald Tribune* quoted Roscoe Drummond,
veteran *Christian Science Monitor* correspondent, as writing, "For
the first time in nineteen years the President of the United States has
begun to bar from his press conference questions he doesn't want asked.
As might be expected, Mr. Truman took this extreme, defensive, unproductive measure in an attempt to erect a shield against the probing questions bearing upon corruption in the Federal government."
But at his first news conference in January there was evidence that
Mr. Truman had been urged to take pointed questions in better humor
even though he did not wish—or intend—to answer them.[32]

In an address in March before 3500 student editors at Columbia
University the President reminded them that he had once been a high
school editor. He also paid his respects to editors and to the press
generally in these words: [33]

"I am very much interested in editors and publishers. It is a very
great responsibility to be an editor of a great newspaper, or a great
periodical, and we have some wonderfully great magazines and newspapers in this country. It is the duty of the editors of these great publications to see that the news is the truth, the whole truth and nothing
but the truth, and these great ones do just that; but we do have
among us some publications who do not care very much for the truth
in the news and sometimes make propaganda out of it, and then write
editorials about it. An editorial written on misrepresentation in the

news and propaganda is just as bad as the foundation on which it rests."

In a news conference on March 20 at Key West, the President said in reply to a question that General Eisenhower was at liberty to return to the United States any time he deemed it safe and proper. Asked how he regarded the general as a politician, Mr. Truman insisted that in his book the general was a military man doing a very able job.[34]

One of the biggest hornets' nests of his career was touched off at his April 17 news conference when Mr. Truman, in reply to a question, seemed to imply that he had the power in an emergency to seize the nation's newspapers and radio stations as he had the steel industry the week before. This was his 300th news conference and not long after he had finally taken himself out of the Presidential race. The question put to him was whether "If it is proper under your inherent powers to seize the steel mills, can you tell us whether, in your opinion, it is proper to seize the newspapers and the radio stations." His reply was that under similar circumstances, the President has to act for whatever is for the best of the country. That is your answer, Mr. Truman said.

A good many editors in Washington to attend the annual ASNE meeting were among the 520 present at the news conference. It was one of them who asked the question. They were quick to register their dissent. E. K. Gaylord, of the *Daily Oklahoman* and Oklahoma City *Times,* declared "If the President could do that, we're pretty close to dictatorship." By a vote of 43 to 36, however, the ASNE convention tabled a resolution to reply to the President.[35] But the American Newspaper Publishers Association in convention the following week in New York City condemned his seizure of the steel industry and declared that it would "resist and defeat" any attempted seizure of the press and radio "by any President."[36] Its resolution was adopted with only four dissenting votes out of nearly 500 publishers present. In Washington, meanwhile, the White House declined to amplify or clarify what the President said earlier.[37] Reaction in the newspapers was prompt and critical. This was reflected in the titles to editorials: "Goodbye to the Constitution?," "Maybe It's Later Than We Thought" and "That Is Your Answer!" Publisher-Editor John S. Knight was prompted to remark in his Editor's Notebook for May 4 on how the Presidency had changed Mr. Truman from a humble beginner "into a testy, opinionated and often reckless Chief Executive."[38]

It is doubtful if the President helped this situation at his April 24 news conference when he called any idea that he believed he could seize the newspapers and radio stations in an emergency a lot of "hooey." Reading slowly from notes, he said such a thought had never occurred to him. He defended the steel seizure as dictated by an emergency. At this conference also the President said he sent a secret ultimatum in 1945 to force Russian troops out of Iran. But within three hours this version was corrected by a White House statement which said that no such ultimatum was ever sent and that Mr. Truman used the term in a "non-technical, layman sense." [39] Former Secretary of State James F. Byrnes also declared that Mr. Truman had sent no such ultimatum. Ludwell Denny, Scripps-Howard foreign editor, called this incident "President Truman's latest foot-in-mouth exhibition." [40]

But if Mr. Truman backed water on the implications of seizing the press and radio facilities he stood his ground on his steel industry seizure. At his May 22 conference he reiterated his belief that neither the courts nor Congress could take away his power to seize fundamental industries in a national emergency. He insisted he did not believe this inherent right was at stake in the steel seizures but promised to abide by the decision of the court. [41] The Supreme Court held against him on June 2.

On the eve of the national convention the President was optimistic over the chances of the Democrats and indifferent or scornful as to the Republicans. At his June 5 conference he said he would attend the Democratic convention after the nominee was chosen. Told that some Republicans had said he was engaged in a "devious plot" to get the nomination for himself, he denied this and declared that such charges usually originated in warped minds. Of a statement the day before by General Eisenhower that the Democrats had been in power too long, the President said that issue was up to the people. [42]

At this June 15 conference, commenting on a flat promise by Senator Taft the day before of a 15 percent tax cut if he got into the White House, Mr. Truman asserted that no President could cut taxes by 15 percent. Despite several recent Eisenhower utterances hardly friendly to the administration, the President reiterated he was still fond of the general and the latter was entitled to his views. [43]

As promised, the President appeared promptly at the Democratic convention following the selection of the Stevenson-Sparkman ticket. He predicted "We are bound to win this election," and in the course of his post-midnight address again paid his respects to the press. He said in part that "these Republicans have nearly all of the newspapers and magazines on their side." He went on: [44]

"The press is controlled by big business. Look at the advertising pages, if you dont believe it. It's always been against President Roosevelt. It has always been against me, and if it was for me, I'd know I was wrong.

"We've gone ahead in spite of it, because the people in five elections in a row have shown they don't pay any attention to what the newspapers tell them. The smart writers—the smart writers can't fool the hard-headed voters of the United States of America . . ."

On August 7 at the first news conference after the convention he said he believed the Democrats had picked the best man—and a winner—in Stevenson. He began the conference by reading two statements, one to the effect that other countries "put us to shame" in turning out the vote. Eleven days later he told 300 members of the CIO Political Action Committee that newspapers as well as Republicans were against Stevenson but that the voters would elect Stevenson anyway. He recalled that 87 percent of the press was "in the other corner" in 1948. He said the Democrats now faced the same situation and "we're going to do exactly again what we did in 1948 and we're going to make them like it." [45]

At a news conference September 11, the President criticized General Eisenhower as a man who was proposing an "isolationist Congress," adding sharply that this would not bring peace. When a reporter said, "That might be construed to mean that it would bring war," he took the correspondent to task. He had not said that, he insisted, adding "Don't misinterpret anything I tell you and don't try to put words in my mouth. I don't like that." [46] At this same conference Mr. Truman declared he did not "give a hoot" what newspapers said about him and the Democratic candidates, provided they printed the truth in their news columns. This followed by three days a blast by Governor Stevenson at Portland, Ore., against the dangers of a "one-party press in a two-party country."

Mr. Truman opened the conference by reading a prepared statement in which he said that in 1948 only 10.3 percent of the nation's 1,769 daily newspapers supported the Democratic party, and "almost all the big circulation magazines were pro-Republican." He added that he did not believe the situation had changed much in four years. He said he agreed with Stevenson's Oregon remark, adding, "I suggest that Americans bear this in mind, and add a dash of salt to every Republican helping of news, especially in those many newspapers and magazines which do not give a fair balance of news between the two major parties." [47]

Mr. Truman suffered a heavy personal loss in the death September 18 of Press Secretary Joseph T. Short from a heart ailment. On September 23 he named Mrs. Short one of his three personal secretaries. On December 18 he made Roger W. Tubby, who had been Short's assistant, Presidential press secretary.

The active part Mr. Truman took in the campaign is well known. It sometimes seemed, however, as though Mr. Truman was the nominee rather than Stevenson. He was confident to the end but after the dimensions of the Republican sweep were known he took the verdict in good grace. In a lengthy public statement he said, in part: "I accept the decision as representing the will of the people, and I shall give my support to the government they have selected. I ask all my fellow citizens to do the same." [48]

His first post-election news conference was held November 20. He had kind words for General Eisenhower and wanted it made clear that the United States had a unified policy. Since this was the first such conference in eight weeks the President and the press were in a kindly mood although there was a barrage of questions. At the end someone asked, "Mr President, have we overlooked anything?" He replied, "Well, if you have, I don't know what it could be." [49] At his December 4 news conference the President let it be known that his "vacation" after leaving office would last at least into June. He disclosed that among many other things he had been offered a job as a columnist but that he would not become one because he had been fussing at columnists for a long time. [50]

At his December 11 conference, however, the Truman temper again got the better of him. He not only rejected suggestions that he hold a conference with Generals Eisenhower and MacArthur but "blasted" both generals. He called the campaign promise that Eisenhower would go to Korea if elected a piece of campaign demagoguery. He was emphatic that MacArthur should have reported to him after the general's return from Japan following his ouster. That is what any decent man would have done, he added. [51] This outburst grew partly out of a remark on Korea by MacArthur on December 5 in an address in New York City. In the interim Eisenhower was en route home from Korea.

Mr. Truman told the correspondents he had traveled 14,000 miles to see MacArthur at Wake Island in 1950 and all he got was a lot of misinformation, namely, that the Chinese would not move into Korea, that a U.S. regular army division could be sent from Korea to Germany by January 1951 and that MacArthur was sure the war was over. What MacArthur said in New York was, "I am confident there is a clear and definite solution to the Korean conflict." Mr. Truman said he could see no good purpose in inviting the generals to a conference but either would be welcome if he had anything he wanted to discuss. Prompted by Press Secretary Tubby, Mr. Truman expressed the hope that some good might come out of the Eisenhower trip and if it did he would be the happiest man in the world.

That same day Republicans assailed the Truman remarks concerning MacArthur as "sour grapes" and a "raucous swan song." One correspondent described the President as being "in about as rough a mood as reporters have seen him in a long time." [52] In its *Review of the Week* on December 12, the New York *Times* said, "Rarely has American history shown an incident so fraught with personal, political and deeply sensitive questions of national policy." One saving grace was that both Eisenhower and MacArthur refused to be drawn into the quarrel, but it was known that the former was greatly displeased over the Truman charge of demagoguery.

The resulting flurry had no effect upon Mr. Truman. At his December 18 conference he insisted that he stood by all the harsh things he had said the week before. But this time the President was in a milder mood in keeping with the Christmas season—he had nothing to add and nothing to take back. As one correspondent phrased it, "Where he was grim and even bitter last week, today the President just laughed in a no-fights-today manner." [53]

The President granted special interviews to a handful of correspondents in the closing days of his administration. In one with Ernest Vaccaro, of the Associated Press, he said that the toughest decision he ever had to make was to send U.S. troops into Korea since it involved the risk of a third World War. Mindful of the criticism to which he had been subjected, he said if he had to do it all over again his major decisions would be the same. He touched on many other topics—the U.S. economy, his future plans, the Point Four program, the Democratic defeat, the charges of corruption, foreign affairs and the atom bombing of Japan. [54]

The one with Merriman Smith, United Press correspondent, drew fire because of a charge that General MacArthur "wanted to involve us in an all-out war in the Far East." He voiced the belief that Russia would welcome a stepped-up war in the Far East so as to have a freer hand in western Europe. The next day MacArthur accused the President of being "inaccurate and misleading." [55]

To a New York *Times* correspondent, Mr. Truman said in part: "If a President makes decisions that are right and for the welfare of the people, it does not make any difference what is said about him while he is alive. The Presidents who have done things, who were not afraid to act, have been the most abused . . . I've been working more than seven and one-half years, walking a tightrope, keeping us out of war—keeping Communism from over-running the free world. I think I have succeeded and I don't think you would want to change that." The *Times* reported that Mr. Truman "said pretty much the same thing" in most of the six personal interviews.[56]

But some took a dim view of the performance. One such critic was David Lawrence, who declared, "There's something pathetic in President Truman's efforts, through a series of belated press interviews to place himself favorably in the perspective of history. For Mr. Truman acts like a floored fighter who doesn't know what the punch was that knocked him out." [57]

To Robert G. Nixon, International News Service correspondent, the President said of the 1952 election that "this was one time that the voters sure shot Santa Claus." He ascribed the Republican victory to three things: glamor and hero worship, McCarthyism and the effect of wholesale character assassination deliberately applied over a long period by the outs, and just plain demagoguery.[58]

Mr. Truman saluted New Year's Day 1953 with a characteristic wish. The Associated Press reported him as hoping the Lord would make him calm enough not to swear at newspapers, but characteristically also he "warmly wished" all the correspondents a happy New Year.

The 324th and final Truman news conference on January 15, 1953 lasted 38 minutes. In that brief time he offered advice to President-elect Eisenhower on the value of such conferences, made announcements or replied to a variety of questions, and told the correspondents, with many of whom he shook hands beforehand, how much he liked them. On specific items he held stoutly to the opinion that the Democrats were still the progressive party, he did not know what he was going to do in the future, and had not made up his mind whether he would write his memoirs. He thanked the reporters for their courtesies to him and told them:[59]

"I want to urge all of you to continue to do your best to dig out the facts and to put them before the people. Naturally, not all of the newspapers agree with me and I do not agree with all of them. But in spite of these differences, I want to make it plain that I think it is important for our democratic system of government that every medium of communication between the citizens and their government, particularly the President, be kept open as far as possible.

"This kind of news conference where reporters can ask any question they can dream up—directly of the President of the United States—illustrates how strong and how vital our democracy is. There is no other country in the world where the chief of state submits to such unlimited questioning; I know, too, from experience that it is not easy to stand up here and try to answer 'off-the-cuff' and all kinds of questions without any advance notice.

"Perhaps succeeding Presidents will be able to figure out inprovements and safeguards in the procedure. I hope they will never cut out the direct line of communication between themselves and the people."

Earlier there had been speculation that President-elect Eisenhower might discontinue the news conferences. In reply to a question, Mr. Truman said firmly he was recommending to his successor that they be continued. He thought they should be held regularly and, while it might help the President to have the questions submitted in writing in advance, for himself he liked the rough and tumble style and declared it was his fault if he "couldn't take care of the questions." He declined to comment on any campaign remarks he had made about General Eisenhower, said he had appreciated the privilege of getting to know the correspondents, that he had tried to give them straight answers, that he had learned from them a lot of things, and that he had got as much "kick" out of their conferences as they had. He wished them all happiness and then, while they applauded, he left. The only correspondent among the 225 present who reportedly did not applaud was Mikhail Federov, of the Russian Tass Agency.

Some 29 hours later Mr. Truman took over the radio and television networks for a farewell fireside chat. In a report tinged with emoion, he reviewed his nearly eight years in the White House, and called for complete public support for his successor to whom he pledged his support.

So on the morrow Harry S. Truman left the White House, attended the Eisenhower inaugural and presently left for Independence. But despite his good intentions he did not step completely or immediately out of the limelight and it was some time before the press began to let him alone. In Kansas City he made the surprising remark that although as President he had announced Russian atomic explosions there was still some doubt in his mind as to whether the Russians had actually produced a workable atomic bomb. This caused some anguish to three members of the Congressional atomic energy committee who issued a statement to the effect that the evidence that Russia had the bomb was "indisputable" and added that the Truman remark was "highly unfortunate." In the first weeks of retirement Mr. Truman was persuaded to comment on a number of matters but finally announced he would have nothing further to say and was mostly as good as his word.

But as John S. Knight observed in his Editor's Notebook,[60] what the ex-President had to say was important. This was in response to a letter from a reader who thought the press should ignore Mr. Truman. Knight said the letter betrayed "so little understanding of the functions of a newspaper," and added that "In our profession, we could not long survive if we printed only those utterances with which we agree, and tossed all contrary opinion into the wastebasket." He predicted that Mr. Truman, "never one to hide his light under a bushel, will stir controversy and animate discussion by his testy comment on the questions of the day. The most recent ex-occupant of the White House was never our favorite President, but as an old hand in the news gathering game, we are always interested in what Harry has to say. And so, we suspect, are a lot of other people."

So to the very end of his term and beyond, Mr. Truman excited interest and controversy. It was greatly to his credit that he steadily maintained good relations with the working press. As with Franklin Roosevelt, his quarrels with the newspapers for the most part were with the publishers and with the press in general. Through eight difficult years he maintained the working relationship which he saw was essential in the public interest. It is for the soundness of this basic political philosophy for which he should be remembered and appraised rather than for occasional outbursts, indignant letters or public castigation of the press. Much of the latter could be charged off to his Missouri temper or simply to politics. Of significance also was the confidence he showed in individual correspondents like Hillman and the six who were favored with the special interviews near the end of his administration. These things were a better measure of the man than the risibilities to which he sometimes yielded.

V

EISENHOWER: FIRST PHASE

Despite a natural unsureness that marked the early months of his administration, Dwight D. Eisenhower in his first year in office made rapid progress in his press relations. Half way through his term there was marked improvement and he was on a generally sound footing with the correspondents. He averaged a news conference about every two weeks, less often than his predecessor, Harry S. Truman, and considerably less often than Franklin D. Roosevelt.

On the whole, the correspondents had few complaints about their relations with Mr. Eisenhower. At one stage a complaint was voiced that a succession of news conferences had favored the afternoon papers and radio stations. The schedule was altered shortly to give the correspondents for the "AM's" a better break.

For his press secretary, the President was fortunate in his choice of James C. Hagerty, a longtime member of the New York *Times* staff. Hagerty and his assistant, Murray Snyder, enjoy the confidence of the correspondents and Hagerty's work in that difficult job has been sound and effective.

Mr. Eisenhower was no stranger to the press when he entered the White House. He dealt with the correspondents variously in North Africa, in the European Theater, as commander of U.S. occupation forces in Germany, as U.S. Army chief of staff, as president of Columbia University, as supreme commander of the Allied Powers in Europe, and especially during the 1952 campaign.

But there was a sharp difference between his status as a ranking military commander, as a university president or even as a Presidential candidate and that of U.S. President. His slightest utterance from the White House might have repercussions around the world.

There were two major developments in the conduct of his conferences. One was the increasing use of the direct quotation, coupled with the President's frequent resort to an official statement on pertinent topics to open his news conference. By so doing he anticipated questions he knew would be forthcoming.

The more spectacular development was the extension of the news conference to the medium of television. The first telecasts were on film which was released after Secretary Hagerty had an opportunity to screen it.   The first news conference so televised occurred January 19, 1955.

The importance of this development can hardly be overestimated. While it was made clear only occasional news conferences would be so filmed and recorded, the important thing was that the precedent was set.   On such occasions the President, as it were, was speaking directly to the American public and, indeed, the world public.

When such a policy, under proper and necessary safeguards, was suggested early in the administration, the reply was that it would not be in the public interest.   On the contrary, it was very much in the public interest.   Another result of this development was to put the newspapers and radio and television on a more equal footing.   If the frequency of the telecasts permitted were to increase or especially if live telecasts were to be permitted, it might change the pattern of newspaper and radio coverage of the conferences.

Two other developments marked the first two years of the Eisenhower relations with the press.   Unlike some of his predecessors, he was slow to use the traditional "No comment" in reply to questions. But several times, because of touchy international relations, he purposely held no news conference so as not to risk adding to the mounting tension.

Like both of his immediate predecessors, President Eisenhower has something of a temper.   There were times at his news conferences when it was an effort to keep it under control. Yet the clenched knuckles, the rising color and the biting emphasis he can employ under such circumstances were evidences of the restrained Eisenhower choler.

Less than a month after election day, the President-elect made history when he took off on a secret flight to Korea to see that war-torn land for himself.   His small party included six reporters and photographers.   Six days later the story was cleared under the dateline "With Eisenhower in Korea, Dec. 5." and the details of the trip began to unfold after the President-elect had left Korea.

In his first eight months in office he held only 14 news conferences. His first news conference occurred February 17, 1953.   This was followed by one more in February, three each in March and April, two in May, only one in June and three in July.   At his first official session with the reporters he altered the normal pattern of such occasions by ending the conference himself.

In other respects, he conformed in the main to his immediate predecessors' practices.   He addressed annual meetings of the American

Society of Newspaper Editors and the American Newspaper Publishers Association. He gave no personal interviews.

In an unprecedented move early in his administration, he helped to obtain the release of William Oatis, Associated Press correspondent, who had been sentenced to 10 years in prison in Czechoslovakia for alleged espionage. The President wrote Czech President Antonin Zapotacky in Oatis' behalf.

To go back, there had been discomfiting rumors that the incoming administration might not hold news conferences regularly. Two weeks before the inauguration, Secretary Hagerty declined to say what the Eisenhower policy would be.[1] Following his election, the President-elect refused to hold news conferences on the grounds that he had no authority until actually in office.

But Secretary Hagerty announced January 21 that Mr. Eisenhower would definitely hold news conferences, probably once a week. He disclosed also that "live" radio and television participation would be permitted in a manner to be determined later. The decision to continue the news conferences won editoral approval throughout the country. To the Columbus *Citizen,* this policy was one that promised public gain. Two days later, it called the news conferences a "Window to the White House."[2] It was announced also about this time that Mrs. Eisenhower would hold news conferences from "time to time," but with political topics taboo.[3]

As with his predecessor, the Eisenhower news conferences were held in the fourth floor conference room of the old State Department building. Secretary Hagerty himself, meanwhile, was holding two press conferences daily—at 10:30 a.m. and at 4 p.m. There had been some grumbling over the administration's slowness in getting the Presidential news conferences under way.

On the eve of the first news conference, Walter Lippmann commented that a triangular relationship existed among the White House, the capitol and the newspapers. Unless the new President, like Franklin D. Roosevelt, managed to make himself the chief source of the most important news, Lippmann warned, the Presidential news conference would deteriorate because of the President's failure to take advantage of it to exercise his leadership.[4]

The new administration made one useful change in news conference procedure. Except for one man each from the State and Defense Departments, government publicity men were excluded to make more room for the working press. During the Truman regime as many as 30 or more government men attended the news conferences.

The initial Eisenhower conference drew more than 250 correspondents, including Mikhail Fedorov, Tass correspondent.[5] The President, after posing briefly for the news photographers, disposed first of the troublesome rumor that he had developed considerable antagonism toward the press. He could not understand, he said, why anyone should feel that he had any hostility toward the press. He had found the press eager only to get at the truth and it had been open-handed and forthright about it. This kind of relationship, he promised, would continue.[6] Next the President brought up five other topics and in the 15 minutes that were left the correspondents got in 18 questions before he left for an appointment. The conference lasted 32 minutes.

In the eyes of Arthur Krock, veteran chief of the New York *Times* Washington bureau, Mr. Eisenhower made an auspicious start. "No President . . . since the beginning of White House press conferences in Woodrow Wilson's time," he wrote, "has given a stronger impression of sincerity, mental integrity, devotion to the basic Constitutional system and amiability that Dwight D. Eisenhower conveyed today. . . ."[7] Bert Andrews, of the New York *Herald Tribune,* also approved. All in all, he wrote, "Mr. Eisenhower stacks up well against his two predecessors. . . . How well he will do when, and if the going gets rougher, time will tell."[8]

As might have been expected, not all of the correspondents agreed. One who had asked a question complained that "He treated me like a G.I.," and a woman reporter said the President talked so long himself that it amounted to an "effective filbuster" and left relatively little time for questions.[9]

At the start of this conference the President was described as "nervous and apprehensive" although he soon took command of the situation. By the end of a month, however, it was being said that he had mastered the news conference technique. Eight days elapsed between his first two news conferences. At his second appearance, he answered 24 questions and expressed a willingness to meet Stalin in an effort to compose East-West differences, but only on the basis of safeguards. He also defended his appointment of Charles E. Bohlen as ambassador to Russia to which Senator McCarthy had objected. This news conference was terminated when a correspondent, reverting to custom, said "Thank you, Mr. President!"[10]

The President began his March 19 news conference with a statement to the effect that the recent shooting down by Russia of U.S.

planes did not necessarily mean any ominous change in Soviet policy. At his March 26 conference the President once more declined to be drawn into a discussion of Senator McCarthy, a position he repeated at his April 2 conference. At the outset of the March 26 conference, press photographers again took pictures of him. He turned to Secretary Hagerty to ask, "Is this going to be a regular thing?" Hagerty replied that this was going to be "the last one." By agreement, the photographers stayed away from his next conference.[11]

In his April 16 address before the ASNE in Washington, the President made a major statement of U.S. foreign policy. He spelled out a 10-point statement in which he outlined a framework for world peace to which all nations could subscribe without endangering their national interests. For his own country, he declared, "We are ready to dedicate our strength to serving the needs, rather than the fears of the world." Publisher John S. Knight called the Eisenhower statement "a moving, momentous pronouncement of faith."[12] The Dayton *Journal Herald* described it as "an impressive performance." *Time* magazine called it "one of the most notable policy statements of U.S. history." The general editorial reaction of the press was highly favorable.

At his sixth news conference, April 23, in the face of "a storm of provocative questions" about the McCarthy issue, the President kept his replies clear and calm. He steadfastly refused to be drawn into the squabble over McCarthyism although he left no doubt as to where he stood. Even that early he was being needled as to Republican prospects in 1954. For this he had a quick and smiling reply: if the Republicans could show a record of progressive accomplishment looking to the interest and welfare of all the people, the party would be back with an enhanced majority.

The Eisenhower news conferences averaged half an hour. The President was always prompt and got immediately to the work in hand. He stood behind a desk and his individual questioners also stood and identified themselves before posing their questions. There was little of the banter that sometimes cropped out under Franklin Roosevelt or Truman.

He began his April 30 conference with a lengthy major statement on the security problem, dealing with military and economic policy. He was asked whether the decision to stretch out NATO's defense build-up represented a change in policy. Thumping his desk, he replied that there must be a continual review of build-up plans. He said the defense budget would be cut but declined to predict the amount.

He opened his May 7 conference with a policy clarifying statement
on the need of the United States to preserve its basic economic and
political freedoms while building up military defenses against global
Communism. The next week the President announced that on May
19 he would make a radio talk to the nation to be followed shortly
by a nationwide television appearance. As to a proposal by Prime
Minister Churchill for a top level international conference, he said
he was ready to do anything but that U.S. self-respect demanded
reasonable assurance that progress could be made.[13]

At his May 28 conference he was asked whether he shared the view
of Senator Taft that "we should forget the United Nations so far as
the Korean war is concerned." His answer was a positive "No!" Then
he gave a calm, well reasoned elaboration. In reply to another question, he maintained that Communist China should not be admitted
to membership in the U.N. under existing conditions.[14]

On the night of June 3, flanked by four cabinet members, the President gave "the fireside chat" he had promised, covering his administration's first month in office. To achieve peace he pledged that the administration would neither tolerate a "new Munich" nor risk a "general war." His appearance was interpreted as an attempt to put
Americans at ease as to U.S. policy in the critical discussions at Pan-
munjom. But, while he gave assurance of his opposition to an expanded war, he made it plain that he would not be a party to any
appeasement of Communism. Public reaction to the program was
favorable on the whole, but there were some dissenters. Columnist
David Lawrence called it inadequate.[15]

With July the Eisenhower administration ended its first six months
in office and there were appraisals of its record to date. At the July
29 conference, the President was asked for a self-appraisal. He said
he would be deceitful if he tried to make out that everything he had
hoped to get done had been accomplished. But he insisted that progress had been made and his word for it was "gradualism."

After a summer respite in Colorado, the news conferences were resumed at the end of September. Reporters and photographers followed the President to Denver but the New York *Herald Tribune* reported
September 27 that he had refused numerous requests for a vacation
press conference. The reporters were briefed from time to time, however, by Secretary Hagerty.

At the September 30 conference Mr. Eisenhower promised to tell
the American public about Russia's ability to manufacture the H-
bomb. Now for the first time he resorted to the "No comment" de-

vice. This grew out of a question as to what qualifications he was looking for in a Secretary of Labor following the resignation of Martin P. Durkin. This conference was notable also because it produced verbal fireworks over the preferential "leak" concerning the nomination of Governor Earl Warren, of California, as chief justice of the Supreme Court.

The President opened the conference by saying he could confirm "something that is certainly by no means news any more." He then officially announced Warren's appointment. Speculation had favored Warren but no confirmation could be had even after Attorney General Brownell returned from California to confer with Warren. But a scant five hours later Brownell had invited five correspondents to his home. He would like to do something for them, he was quoted as saying, because they had been good to him. He then had told them about the impending Warren appointment, but strictly "not for attribution." The papers these correspondents represented had featured the story the next day.

At the September 30 news conference, Raymond P. Brandt, St. Louis *Post-Dispatch* correspondent, demanded of the President, "Is it going to be the policy of this administration to leak such important news to friendly newspapers?" (Soon after he took office the President had set up a strict "no leak" policy for members of his staff.) His reply to Brandt's question was that he had trusted subordinates who might occasionally leak stories when they felt they should. The President added that he would try to be fair to the press but if the correspondents had any complaints they should be submitted to Secretary Hagerty.

The next day angry reporters confronted Secretary Hagerty. They asked whether he or the President knew in advance that Brownell planned to leak the story. His reply was hardly calculated to sweeten their tempers. The Associated Press reported him to have answered hotly, "It is none of your business, but the answer is no." [16] Since it involved White House news policies, it was understandable that the reporters felt strongly that it was their business. Nor was it any wonder that some felt that the administration's press relations had deteriorated. John O'Donnell, New York *Daily News* writer, commented acidly that "The education of Dwight D. Eisenhower in the sweet uses of publicity now turns out to be a complete bust." [17]

A week later, at his next conference, the President was described as showing "a new capability for fencing with the press." Earlier, it was pointed out, he had nearly always given forthright replies to questions. On one as to balancing the budget he said that with any administration like his budget balancing would always be a goal but he was not going to say that the budget was going to be balanced on July 1, 1955. On a question as to the chances of a non-aggression agreement with Russia and the report that Adlai Stevenson had brought him a personal appeal from Prime Minister Churchill for an international conference, he admitted only that the possibility of an agreement was being studied and that he had received personal greetings from an old friend.

The correspondents continued to press the President as to his intentions with respect to politics. At his October 21 conference he was asked whether he would take the stump in the critical House and Senate election campaigns in 1954. Once more he declined to spell out the details. As President he was greatly interested in what happened to the makeup of the Senate and the House of Representatives, yet he did not intend to make his office an agency to serve partisan politics. It was his idea that while he was elected by only a part of the population he was President of all the people. He intended, therefore, not to become entangled in partisan contests on the local level. Columnist David Lawrence, commenting on this conference, wrote that the President was "beginning to handle himself at his press conferences more and more like a veteran." [18] This was echoed by Roscoe Drummond, of the New York *Herald Tribune*, who remarked that "Even though he may not always enjoy it—and who would?—President Eisenhower is meeting the press with increasing skill, candor and good will." [19]

Not everyone agreed. On a television program a few days later, Raymond P. Brandt, of the St. Louis *Post-Dispatch* Washington bureau, argued that the administration's relations with the press had worsened. Press Secretary Hagerty, on the same program, contended that the reporters were getting the news "more fairly and more accurately than they did in the past administration." [20]

The questions on politics continued. Despite what he had said the week before, Mr. Eisenhower intimated October 28 that he might take the stump in 1954 for a GOP program in Congress, if not for individual candidates. A week later, he said that, while he was not pleased with some of the results, he had "lost skirmishes before." [21]

On November 6, the President issued an order which modified a controversial policy of the Truman administration. The order, announced by Attorney General Brownell, eliminated the "restricted" category for classifying government data as harmful to national security if made public. The new order was to be effective December

15. It also set up a system for receiving complaints from newsmen and others, eliminated document classifying authority from 28 agencies, and among other things defined what information was to be classified. The White House said the order was designed to attain "a proper balance between the need to protect information important to the defense of the United States, and the need for citizens of this democracy to know what their government is doing." [22]

The November 11 conference, relatively brief, was very tempestuous. It began calmly enough with a few Eisenhower remarks about Armistice Day and several other matters. What started the "deluge," as one correspondent called it, was whether the President would give his opinion of ex-President Truman having been subpoenaed by the House Un-American Affairs Committee. Raymond P. Brandt, of the St. Louis *Post-Dispatch*, started to say that he had a list of questions, but the President recognized Merriman Smith, of the United Press, who asked the first question about Mr. Truman.

After another reporter got in a question, Brandt tried again. Before he posed a question the President, flushing, told him, "Just a minute," he might ask one question but was not sure it was customary for one reporter to ask a number of questions. Brandt then asked whether the President knew in advance of Attorney General Brownell's recent speech in Chicago regarding Harry Dexter White and whether he was consulted as to plans "to bring the White story out." Brandt also inquired whether he thought Congress should subpoena a Supreme Court justice (meaning Clark). Mr. Eisenhower replied that he thought there were other ways of handling the situation. Brandt asked further whether "the Administration's action in virtually putting a label of traitor on a former President is likely to damage our foreign relations." According to the *Herald Tribune* account, this brought "another angry glare from the President," who stoutly rejected the premise and would not answer the question. Others tried their hand at related questions and the harassed President finally declared flatly that "he was going to answer his last question right now on this subject for this morning at least," and then repeated in substance what he had said as to Brownell's part in the matter.

James B. Reston, of the New York *Times* called this "the stormiest White House news conference of recent years." Robert J. Donovan, of the *Herald Tribune,* described it as "the severest test" Mr. Eisenhower "had had to meet at a press conference" and wrote that "at times the President appeared to be restraining his temper with conscious effort." The conference got wide attention in the press. It was made the subject of a special article in the *Nieman Reports* in which the full text of the unofficial transcript was reprinted.[23] The Cleveland *Plain Dealer* editorially deplored the attitude of some correspondents for indicating "contemptuous disbelief of some of the President's statments." [24] Harold Callender, Paris correspondent of the New York *Times,* commented that abroad few would believe that the President "subjected himself to an incisive cross-examination by reporters who were 'better briefed than he was on the answers to a cannonade of questions they shot at him,' as the Manchester *Guardian*'s correspondent described it." Callender pointed out that no European premier or foreign minister "would dream of according the press the privilege accorded to it by President Eisenhower." [25]

The next Eisenhower news conference was less stormy but still had elements of tension. The recurrent question of the attitude of the administration toward McCarthyism came up. "Flushing, the President replied abruptly," the Associated Press reported, "that he was ready to take the judgment of the assembled reporters on the matter. He swung his glasses and bit off his words in such a staccato way that several reporters asked him to repeat them." He "went on to say that he did not like the word 'McCarthyism' and was not sure what the term implied." [26]

Two more Eisenhower news conferences rounded out 1953. The first, held December 2, produced some minor fireworks. The President defended Attorney General Brownell and without mentioning Senator McCarthy by name upheld Secretary of State Dulles, who the day before had rebuked McCarthy for criticizing U.S. foreign policy. The second, December 16, was noteworthy in that for the first time the entire conference was recorded on a tape which was made available to radio and television networks.

The President sketched his plans at his December 16 conference for an intensive three-day series of legislative conferences to draft "a progressive, dynamic program" to be laid before Congress in January. This news conference was notable because it was the first time newspapers were permitted to quote a President directly without limitation. Mr. Eisenhower called this "a Christmas present" to the correspondents and the public. Press Secretary Hagerty termed it a first step toward broadening the coverage of Eisenhower news conferences. He said recordings of future conferences would be released from time to time. All major radio networks broadcast the recording, somewhat trimmed down, while two television networks used excerpts against background films of previous presidential news conferences.[27]

The change in policy was hailed favorably. Edward R. Murrow,
CBS news analyst, said the new policy "draws the president and the
people closer together, and increases interest in public affairs." But
he asked whether "if tape recordings of press conferences are going
to be broadcast often, are they not going to force the President to
put a curb on himself?" [28]

The year 1954 produced a number of Presidential news conferences
(a) at which the Eisenhower temper was sorely tried, (b) at which
momentous news was made, and (c) at which further changes were
made in procedure. By the end of his first year in office he had held
24 press conferences, had made history by permitting the first radio
broadcast of an entire news conference, and had taken the pubilc further into partnership by arranging for a televised session with some
members of his cabinet.

Opinions differed somewhat on the net results of his press relations
but the general reaction was good and the improvement noticeable.
Following his January 13, 1954, conference, Andrew Tully, a Scripps-
Howard writer, remarked that "President Eisenhower still may not
enjoy his press conferences as Harry Truman did, but he's beginning
to feel at home in them." [29] This was echoed by Roscoe Drummond,
of the New York *Herald Tribune,* who observed that "Every Presidential press conference strengthens the conviction of most Washington
correspondents that, while there is not a new Eisenhower in the
White House, there is quite a different Eisenhower in the White
House from a year ago." Drummond added that the President was
"handling himself with force and poise and skill." [30]

But when a reporter remarked at his January 27 news conference
that "Some people have characterized your legislative program as an
extension of the New Deal," the President replied somewhat sharply
that the best answer to that was to look at the budget. Specifically, he
pointed out that in the area of human relationships his administration
believed in being what "we would normally call liberal, and when we
deal with the economic affairs of this country, we believe in being con-
servative." [31] At his February 3 news conference he called for a halt to
any further spread of hysterical fear in connection with U.S. possession
of atomic weapons through bombastic statements. A week later
he emphasized that it would be a tragedy for the U.S. to become involved in the "hot war" then in progress in Indo-China, a pronouncement that was hailed with relief in Congress.

During the fore part of 1954 there was some fear that a recession
was under way and there was some criticism that the administration

was slow to meet this danger. At his February 17 news conference the President said if employment failed to improve in March, it would be a warning of economic trouble calling for government action. Drumming a desk top for emphasis, he gave assurance that if a major downturn appeared likely he would not hesitate to use every resource available to head it off.

The issue of "McCarthyism" persisted and the President was forced to meet it after a fashion. At his March 3 news conference, he lashed at "disregard of the standards of fair play" in Congressional investigations and emphasized that no one in the armed forces had to submit "to any kind of personal humiliation" before investigating committees. This turned on the recent row between Senator McCarthy and Brig. Gen. Ralph Zwicker. The President conceded that the Army had made "serious errors" but was taking steps to avoid such mistakes in the future.

A week later he again gave assurance against fears of U.S. involvement in a shooting war in Indo-China. In reply to a question, Mr. Eisenhower said: "There is going to be no involvement of America in war unless it is a result of the constitutional process that is placed upon Congress to declare it." James Marlow, Associated Press columnist, wrote that this statement "may be remembered long after the present hubbub over Sen. McCarthy is forgotten." [32] At this conference the President uttered the strongest criticism he had spoken to date against McCarthy. A day earlier, Senator Ralph E. Flanders, of Vermont, had denounced McCarthy for "doing his best to shatter" the Republican party. The President declared that Flanders had rendered a "service." At his March 17 news conference, the President defended Army Secretary Stevens in his continuing row with Senator McCarthy. To quote the Associated Press, "Eisenhower, with red-faced irritation he made no apparent effort to conceal, made it plain he is sick and tired" of such controversies. [33]

A giant hydrogen device was set off March 1 under U.S. auspices in the Pacific. At his March 24 news conference the President expressed the belief that U.S. scientists might have gotten more than they bargained for. He took the unprecedented step at his March 31 conference of having Lewis L. Strauss, Atomic Energy Commission chairman, present to read and discuss a statement on the recent Pacific bomb tests. Strauss said the tests had increased the U.S. military potential "enormously." [34]

The President made a major address April 22 in New York at the annual convention of the American Newspaper Publishers Association in which he declared this country must take the lead in developing a genuine understanding among the peoples of the world that would lead to lasting peace. "If this is not to be the age of atomic hysteria and horror," he declared, "we must make it an age of international understanding and cooperative peace." He urged newspaper publishers to give emphasis to the things that unite the American people equal to that which they give to things that divide them.[35]

Columnist Walter Lippmann took exception to the President's remarks. He interpreted them as having reference to administration complaints that "the newspapers have made McCarthy too powerful by giving too much space and too many headlines to him." As an "old newspaper man," Lippmann went on, he believed McCarthy's charges were "news which cannot be suppressed or ignored" and the only real "balance" to be had was "by news about the truth or falsity of those charges." As a matter of fact, the columnist added, "Gen. Eisenhower himself has a heavy responsibility for the things he complains about." [36]

At his April 29 news conference the President gave renewed assurance that the United States would not get into a war without a declaration by Congress. But the climax of this conference came when in a "scene unique in Presidential press conference history," Mr. Eisenhower, "nearly speechless with emotion"—to quote the *Herald Tribune* account—stalked from the conference room upon being asked what he thought of allegedly preferential treatment the Army accorded Pvt. G. David Schine, former consultant to Senator McCarthy. To quote further:[37]

"There was a silence. The President drew up his shoulders and clenched his hands together, and when he answered, it was in a deeply husky voice.

"He said he trusted that the reporters would excuse him for declining to talk at all about that . . . He just hoped, he said, it would be concluded very quickly. That's all, he said. He left the room."

An explanation of what lay behind this was offered by the *Herald Tribune* Washington bureau staff. It read, in part: "A feeling of deep frustration lay behind the angry emotion President Eisenhower showed at last week's press conference over the McCarthy-Army hearings. After sixteen months in office, the situation is the very opposite of what the President hoped it would be. Republicans are in bitter conflict over the Schine investigation. The Eisenhower program is getting second billing in Congress . . ." [38]

The May 5 news conference was comparatively quiet but that of

May 12 produced more fireworks over McCarthy. A correspondent remarked that the senator had just testified that an Army intelligence officer had supplied him with classified material. The President recalled that at the last news conference he had said he was thinking of taking a vacation from replies to questions dealing with McCarthy, that he would not comment now on this one as to McCarthy, but it was reprehensible for an Army officer to have supplied confidential FBI data without authorization.

On May 16 an order came from the White House to Defense Secretary Wilson against divulging consultations of the executive branch. At his May 19 news conference the President made it clear he had "no intention whatsoever of relaxing or rescinding the order" as a "very moderate and proper division of powers between the executive and the legislative . . ." McCarthy had attacked the order as an "iron curtain." [39] The order grew out of a meeting January 21 to decide whether the Army should produce the records of its Loyalty Screening Board as demanded by the McCarthy subcommittee. To a question as to whether he had any advice for the South on the recent Supreme Court decision against segregation, Mr. Eisenhower urged the South to meet it with calmness and reasonableness. On May 25 the White House announced that the President would hold no news conference that week and Secretary Hagerty declined to give a reason. On May 28, the administration, through Hagerty at the direction of Attorney General Brownell, flatly disputed a claim by Senator McCarthy that it was the duty of federal workers to tell Congress what they might know about Communism, treason or other crimes. [40]

Meanwhile an impression was growing that the administration was suffering from a bad press. The Alsops, for example, observed that the administration had done much better than it appeared to be doing but had failed to put its best foot forward by explaining its policies frankly. [41] Walter Lippmann similarly described the President as being in trouble as a result of inept handling of such issues as those involving Senator McCarthy and J. Robert Oppenheimer, the nuclear scientist. In the same vein, John S. Knight remarked that the Scripps-Howard Newspapers had lately given the President good advice in urging that he provide the Republican party with the leadership it needed, and particularly that it was "high time" Mr. Eisenhower should "start swinging" in the McCarthy controversy. Knight observed that the President knew how to lead and demanded, in effect, why doesn't he do it? [42] Raymond Moley noted that scrutiny of the published text of White House news conferences disclosed "a serious lack of efficiency

and many a missed opportunity for more and more specific enlight-
ment of the public concerning the government of the United States." [43]
Shortly after this Marquis Childs wrote, in effect, that the "Ike-Press
Honeymoon Appears Ended." [44]

During June, July and August the President held eleven more news
conferences before going to Denver on vacation. All of these sessions
made news but only a few were particularly noteworthy. At his June
2 meeting he said he had reached no decision on any step such as a
possible Congressional resolution to authorize U.S. intervention in
Southeast Asia. In a sort of indirect reply to Senator McCarthy he emphasized also that the administration was fighting Communism at
home on "a 24-hour, seven-days-a-week, 52-weeks-a-year" basis.
But with a look of annoyance he turned aside further questions on the
McCarthy issue.[45] At the June 16 conference he insisted he was giving
no thought as to whether he would seek reelection in 1956.

The question of admitting Red China to the United Nations came
up at the July 7 news conference and Mr. Eisenhower declared he was
unalterably opposed to it under present conditions. But he was not
ready to say that this country would withdraw if Red China was admitted, thus taking issue with Senator Knowland and others. At
his July 21 news session he said that despite its unsatisfactory features
he welcomed the end of fighting in Indo-China and hoped that the
truce would lead promptly to a Southeast Asia agreement to check
further Communist aggression there. He declined to take a position
on a resolution by Senator Flanders, of Vermont to censure Senator
McCarthy. On the President's performance at recent news conferences
columnist Ruth Montgomery remarked that he was "amazing the
Washington press corps by the openhandedness of his replies."[46]

Yet at his August 4 news conference the President again let his
emotions get the upper hand over a question about a derogatory letter
from ex-Secretary of War Harry Woodring which Senator McCarthy
had put into the *Congressional Record* about General George C. Marshall. Mr. Eisenhower warmly defended Marshall as a great patriot
and declared that such attacks were a "sorry reward" for a lifetime of
patriotic service. In another pregnant statement the President expressed anxiety over the harmful effects of the McCarthy issue upon
the Republican party and indicated that he might have to deal with
the situation, but not as to what he might do. He also voiced the
belief there was too much talk of U.S. "leadership" and it would be
better to view this country's role as that of a "good partner." [47]

The next week the President, at his conference, rejected suggestions for a diplomatic break with Russia and labeled the idea of a preventive war as unthinkable. In respect to the former he disagreed strongly with those who were urging reorganization of the United Nations as an agency opposed to the Soviets. He expressed himself as amused over conjecture as to whether he would run again in 1956. At his final news conference on August 17 before leaving for Colorado, the President made it plain that any Communist invasion of Formosa would have to be over the U.S. 7th Fleet which had orders to defend the island.

Recent developments in the White House news conferences brought some diversity of opinion as to their status. To Roscoe Drummond, of the New York *Herald Tribune,* Eisenhower had "mastered the technique of the press conference" and was "beginning to use it effectively in his own interests." [48] Drummond quoted other unnamed correspondents as agreeing that the President was not only calmer and more adroit but was using the conferences as "an instrument of Presidential leadership." But the veteran David Lawrence argued that the conferences not only were not improving but were doing greater injury to the President and his party as well as to U.S. influence abroad. Much of this harm, he explained, was because Mr. Eisenhower often failed to get the full story behind the questions he got at news conferences. In domestic matters, Lawrence added, the President "stumbled" leaving "ambiguities" in the trail of his answers to political questions. The remedy, in Lawrence's opinion, lay in the need for better teamwork between the President and his advisers. [49] Yet James B. Reston, of the New York *Times,* found the President now "clearly at ease even with the most controversial questions" and felt that the news conference, "which used to be a crisis, is now seen at the White House as an opportunity." [50]

During the President's stay in Denver there were no formal news conferences but he had rare informal contacts with the correspondents as, for example, the day after his televised speech on the record of the 83rd Congress. As usual Mr. Eisenhower was followed by the press, so that even former President Hoover complained that "the press no longer has any respect for the privacy of the President in his fishing." Mr. Hoover had just been the President's guest on a fishing trip. On September 13 Mr. Eisenhower briefed the reporters on a meeting in Denver of the National Security Council at which he said the U.S. would continue to defend its vital interests "wherever they arise." He declined to answer questions. On September 29 from Denver he issued a statement in connection with National Newspaper

Week that "no institution is more necessary to our way of life than a free press."

After his return to Washington the biennial election was the chief topic of interest. On October 25 further communications history was made with the telecast of a full cabinet meeting (at night) at which Secretary Dulles reported on negotiations for a European defense agreement. Two days later, at his first fall news conference, the President was plagued with questions on the impending election. On one as to whether voter apathy was due to any "disenchantment with the program of the last two years," Mr. Eisenhower, to quote the Cleveland *Plain Dealer* account, "never cracked a smile. Instead, he seemed to have increasing trouble controlling his temper . . ." [51] In reply to another inquiry, he declined to predict the outcome of the election.

As expected, the Congressional elections went against the Republicans although not as heavily as predicted. At his news conference the morning after the election interest centered in the results then available. The very first question was whether he saw "any disapproval to administration policies in the Republican loss of the House." His answer was to the point: "No, I don't." Another question was whether the results affected "whatever thinking you may have about 1956"—a reference to the Presidential election two years away. His reply: "Well, certainly it hasn't so far," adding that he never tried "to predict too far in advance" even with respect to himself. [52]

At his November 10 news conference, he was asked about the recent shooting down of a U.S. reconnaissance plane off the northeast tip of Japan. His answer was that rather than use its planes as sitting ducks the United States should have them accompanied when necessary by fighter escort. His manner was anything but belligerent although in effect it served notice on Russia—and the world—as to U.S. intentions. At his November 23 conference he said the greatest mistake this country could make would be to lose sight of Russia's plans for world revolution and domination. But he said again that the United States was for a Big Four conference if there was concrete proof of Russia's sincerity.

In December, he held three news conferences. At that of December 2 he made it plain that the United States would not be goaded into any hasty, angry action in the cold war. He declared also that the Republican party must follow a moderate but progressive course and held the door open to future cooperation with Senator Knowland, of California, who often favored more drastic action. The next week he voiced the opinion that the free world's fears of a global war had diminished in the last four years and that the last year had brought considerable accomplishment in his "atoms for peace" proposal. But again he refused to be drawn into any discussion of Senator McCarthy who the day before charged the President with weakness toward Communism. On December 15 he said he would ask the new Congress to postpone tax cuts that had been scheduled for April 1 next. But he dodged direct comment on a radio remark by Press Secretary Hagerty that it would be foolhardy for the Republicans to fail to nominate Mr. Eisenhower for a second term. Roscoe Drummond, of the New York *Herald Tribune,* called the President's handling of his December 2 news conference "the most impressive, forceful and decisive exercise of Presidential leadership since Mr. Eisenhower has been in the White House . . . He did not thump his desk. He did not raise his voice—but his words carried around the whole free world." [53]

Merriman Smith, veteran White House correspondent, at the close of the year wrote that "President Eisenhower's press conference technique seems to be improving steadily." After 58 news conferences since taking office, he added, the "tenseness he showed in the early months has markedly disappeared." But he went on: "He still is the most difficult president in recent years to follow on pencil and paper. This is due to his speed of speech, plus what has been described as his 'circular' sentence construction." The Eisenhower temper of his Army days, Smith went on, "rarely shows itself before reporters." And so far he had exhibited none of "the face-to-face criticism, scorn, and occasional namecalling" in which Franklin Roosevelt and Truman sometimes indulged toward reporters. "On occasion, a question will anger him," Smith continued, "and his reply will show it. But his reply usually is directed to the question, not the questioner . . ." [54]

To round out his first two years in office, Mr. Eisenhower held two news conferences in January 1955—on January 12 and 19. The latter was particularly noteworthy in that it was the first Presidential news conference at which television and newsreel cameramen were authorized to make sound movies. This was a landmark in White House news conferences. Negatively, it was significant that because of the delicacy of the situation involving Formosa and the Chinese Reds, the President purposely held no news conference on January 26 because he did "not want to have anything more to say" on his Formosa defense policy while it was under consideration in Congress. [55]

The January 19 conference was important not so much for what was said as because in essence it changed the pattern of Presidential news conferences. In addition to film for television and newsreel cameras permission was given for the first time for "still" photographers to operate during the conference. Secretary Hagerty intimated that subject to certain limitations this practice would be followed at future news conferences. He explained the innovation to the correspondents as follows: "This is being done so that all media of information can cover presidential news conferences, and so the people of our country can not only read the reports of the conferences but can hear and see the discussions the President has with you gentlemen." [56] The White House, reserved the right, through Hagerty, to "edit" the sound movies. In the case of this first such conference, the edited film was released in time to be telecast over nationwide networks early that evening. Hagerty was asked whether the "editing" did not amount to censorship, but his answer was "Not at all. . . . We want the White House to remain in control of the spoken word of the President." [57] This was still not live television but it marked a distinct advance over anything permitted previously. For the first time the public was in a position to feel that it, too, was "present." The N.Y. *Herald Tribune* called the change "a big contribution to public enlightenment." [58]

This particular conference also marked the half-way mark of the administration. In response to a question, Mr. Eisenhower said that the Presidency was a mixed blessing, but defended his record. Among other things he said the Tachen Islands were not essential to the defense of Formosa and added that he would like to see the United Nations attempt to arrange a cease-fire between Nationalist China and Communist China. Asked to tell something of his hopes "for the next two or maybe even next six years," he commented that it "looks like a loaded question." This was his 58th news conference.

By a coincidence, four days before the filmed news conference, *Editor & Publisher* published an analysis of the Eisenhower news conferences. The article, by S. Richard Brooks, accounted for 55 news conferences, attended on the average by 200 reporters, with a total of more than 2,500 questions put to the President. Brooks broke down the questions asked into 11 categories. The greatest number of questions on any one thing turned on Senator McCarthy, followed by Indo-China, and the biennial election. Merriman Smith, veteran United Press correspondent, led with 55 questions, followed by Raymond P. Brandt, St. Louis *Post-Dispatch*, with 53. Others in the first ten were Sarah McClendon, El Paso *Times;* May Craig, Gannett (Maine) Newspapers; Marvin Arrowsmith, Associated Press; Chalmers Roberts and Edward Folliard, Washington *Post and Times Herald;* Robert Clark, INS; Anthony Leviero, New York *Times;* and Richard Wilson, Cowles

Publications. The total box score, Brooks wrote, represented "a great victory for the people's right to know." [59]

In his first two years of Presidential news conferences the consensus was that Mr. Eisenhower on the whole had acquitted himself well, a judgment supported by the record. Despite a show of temper now and then he was generally at ease with his questioners, earned their good will and respect by the frankness of his answers and particularly because he almost never resorted to the old device of "No comment." If his news conferences were not as frequent or as spectacular as those of his two predecessors they were generally fruitful and Mr. Eisenhower conducted himself with good humored dignity.

He obviously tried to give such information as he had and often began his conference with statements pertinent to the moment or which anticipated questions sure to be asked. When he did not know the answer, he said so frankly and often promised to get it if he could. In particular, the filming of his news conferences put the Presidential practice at a new high level. By the same token there was a definite increase in the direct quotation of the President's own words. It was still the White House prerogative to give permission for the direct quote but the changing nature of the relationship necessarily reduced the longstanding practice of indirect attribution. As never before, the Presidential news conference at the start of the third year of the Eisenhower administration was becoming a picture window through which the public could see the President. This was in the basic interest of the public's right to know and, in respect to the executive, gave the U.S. public an advantage unequaled anywhere in the world.

EISENHOWER: SECOND PHASE

For the first time in nearly a quarter of a century there has been an extended partial vacuum in the flow of news from the White House or, more accurately, between its occupant and the correspondents as a result of the heart attack President Eisenhower suffered in the early morning hours of September 24, 1955. Paradoxically at no other period of his entire life has Mr. Eisenhower had such extensive and unremitting press, radio and television news coverage as during the three months following his cardiac "accident." Nor did any of his predececsors have such complete and authoritative reporting of a personal illness—Wilson or Harding, for example—as Mr. Eisenhower has had. Chief credit for this record goes to James C. Hagerty, the President's efficient and highly respected press secretary.

The fact remains, however, that for the first time in years the White House correspondents have been cut off for a considerable period from their accustomed first-hand contacts with the President. As the new year began it was nearly five months and might run longer. The correspondents had seen him from time to time, especially following his return to his Gettysburg farm in mid-November. But the last previous White House news conference was that of August 4, 1955 in Washington just before the President left for his annual vacation in Colorado. Under his practice there were no news conferences during his stay in or near Denver. The most hopeful outlook was for a resumption of the conferences in Washington in the early winter of 1956.

In the interim Secretary Hagerty continued to be the principal link between the President and the correspondents. Hagerty won the undying gratitude of the latter by the thoroughness and frequency of his own news conferences, both in Denver and at Gettysburg. But with all respect to him, his authority is limited and the correspondents, while accepting the necessity for the situation, missed the periodic give-and-take with the President himself, a solid custom developed to their great mutual advantage—but especially to that of the U.S. public—since Franklin D. Roosevelt took office in March 1933.

Until the Eisenhower heart attack occurred there were only two periods between 1932 and 1955 during which somewhat similar partial vacuums developed in respect to direct Presidential news. One was during the closing months of the Hoover administration when relations between Mr. Hoover and the working press left much to be desired. The other occurred at times during World War II when Mr. Roosevelt was out of the country or was otherwise inaccessible to the press.

In the closing months of Mr. Hoover's term relations between him and the newspapermen worsened steadily. From June 1 to mid-September, 1932, he saw the correspondents only eight times, and in the next 10 weeks all official White House news came from Press Secretary Joslin who refused to enlarge upon any announcement.[1] Not only were there no press conferences during the campaign in which Mr. Hoover fought a losing battle, but he did not resume them after the election. A press conference was announced for November 18, 1932 but it was canceled without explanation and the same thing recurred a week later. As a result, Herbert Hoover ended his term with relations with the working press more strained than in any President's term within the memory of White House correspondents.

There were times also during Franklin Roosevelt's third term when, because of situations incident to the critical war years, he was temporarily out of touch with the press. At the time of his historic Atlantic Charter meeting with Churchill in August 1941 off the Maine coast the connection was completely severed for 13 days as far as U.S. correspondents were concerned.[2] They were quite irritated when they learned that accredited British correspondents accompanied Churchill.

There was irritation also over the conditions imposed upon the correspondents at the time of the Quebec, Cairo and Tehran conferences. When Roosevelt saw Churchill at Quebec they finally met the press but no questions were permitted. At Cairo, Tehran and at Yalta the correspondents were held at arm's length. At Cairo they were kept from the scene of the sessions by barbed wire and bayonets. During the war Roosevelt was necessarily away from Washington from time to time on official business, but he disappeared once for a month and it was learned later that he had been at Bernard Baruch's estate in South Carolina for his health.[3]

Except at the very outset of Mr. Eisenhower's illness the flow of information concerning his ailment and his progress left nothing to be desired. Secretary Hagerty was away on a brief vacation when the heart attack occurred, but returned to his job promptly. The initial announcement of Mr. Eisenhower's illness was to the effect that he had a mild digestive upset. But a dozen hours later, by which time the

President had gone to Fitzsimons Army Hospital in Denver, the true
nature of his illness was bared. From that time on both the White
House secretariat and the medical men immediately responsible put
themselves out to make every scrap of information available promptly.⁴

This was especially true of Dr. Paul Dudley White, the Boston
cardiac specialist, who was flown to Denver on September 25 and who
made further trips there and to Gettysburg to check up on his distinguished patient. Dr. White not only made detailed reports as to the
President's exact condition and progress but, through arrangements
made by Secretary Hagerty, submitted himself to the correspondents'
question-and-answer routine. This not only gave them authoritative
information straight from the top authority but was highly reassuring
to the public.

Only one minor incident involving the communications media marred the early weeks of the President's convalescence. This occurred
when an over-anxious newsreel cameraman for one of the major broadcasting networks flew in a helicopter fairly close to the roof of the
hospital in an evident effort to get pictures of the President sunning
himself on the eighth floor terrace there. As it happened, Mr. Eisenhower had gone inside shortly before the helicopter appeared. The
Cincinnati *Enquirer,* in a rather sharp editorial, declared that it could
not imagine anyone ordering pictures of the President "under circumstances that might endanger his life." It set down the effort as
"merely the work of an overly eager beaver," and asserted, "No part
of the media of public information wants a picture of President Eisenhower that badly." ⁵

On October 25, a month after he entered the hospital, Mr. Eisenhower posed for the news cameras on the hospital terrace, but under
limited conditions. The 10 photographers admitted were under in-
structions to work quickly, to give no "shouted orders," and to come
no closer than 12 feet to the distinguished patient. One correspondent,
Garnett D. Horner, of the Washington *Star,* accompanied the cameramen to give a first hand report of the occasion for the benefit of all
the correspondents.⁶

From the first the President made satisfactory progress and the official reports, initially four times a day, were encouraging and reassuring. On November 11 he flew back to Washington and a warm welcome and then, after a brief stay, went to his farm home at Gettysburg. A temporary executive office was set up for him in the Gettysburg postoffice, while a nearby hotel ballroom was turned over to the
corps of correspondents. The President waved to reporters as he ar-

rived for work periods at the postoffice but Secretary Hagerty continued to be the main source of news about the President, his family, and their plans and activities. Occasionally the correspondents questioned members of the cabinet and of Congress or politicians who visited the President, but for the most part these contacts were not very productive.

The unavoidable extension of this hiatus in the relations between the President himself and the news and camera men into 1956 increased speculation and suggestions (1) as to the possibility of a resumption of the news conferences, and (2) for some means of supplementing the contacts with Secretary Hagerty. This latter suggestion was in no sense a criticism of Hagerty—on the contrary, there was nothing but praise and gratitude for his unstinting efforts to keep the press informed on the smallest details. But this did not lessen the desire to establish more or less regular contacts for news purposes with some other spokesman for the President and the administration.

In approximately 36 months in office Mr. Eisenhower had held only 75 news conferences. (By contrast, his predecessor, Harry S. Truman, had 256 such conferences in his first six years in that office; this averaged out about one every two weeks for Mr. Eisenhower to five every six weeks for Mr. Truman.) One important change by Mr. Eisenhower early in 1955 was to permit the live filming and sound recording of White House news conferences. This made it possible for millions of citizens as well as the correspondents to see and hear what went on at such occasions. Eighteen such conferences had been recorded up to the time of the President's illness, of which 10 had been released in their entirety.[7] The impact of this development on the whole range of White House public relations was tremendous and its importance could not be overestimated. This made it doubly hard for the correspondents and cameramen when the President's illness shut off virtually all first hand contacts with Mr. Eisenhower indefinitely.

With the major question of whether the President would consent to run for re-election still unsettled as the new year began, some were pessimistic enough to foresee the possibility that he might not even resume his news conferences.[8] The majority of the correspondents hoped, however, that he would do so as soon as his health permitted although this might be several months off. Secretary Hagerty set this doubt and speculation at rest December 21 when he announced that the President planned to resume his news conferences perhaps as early as mid-January or whenever he got "back in the regular routine of his office." [9] This would make the gap of the "vacuum" a minimum of five months.

The long drought was partly broken when on January 8 the President took part in a rather impromptu news conference at Key West, Fla., where on medical advice he had spent 12 days just relaxing. The conference came about when the President, overhearing the correspondents' interest in his progress toward recovery, offered to chat with them just before boarding his plane to return to Washingtin. About 50 newsmen attended the conference, including a crew which filmed and recorded the question-and-answer session for later use on television and radio. Although it had been indicated that Mr. Eisenhower would discuss only "the immediate future," he replied freely to questions bearing upon his political intentions.

Perhaps the most important single question he answered was whether he had made up his mind as to running for re-election. On this he replied: "No. If it were, I would say so right here this second. But my mind is not fixed to such an extent that it can't be changed." A majority of the correspondents present who were polled took this to mean that he would not run again.

The President flew back to the White House that afternoon to resume, as he put it at the news conference, "the full duties of the presidency" the next morning. Steps were already in motion, meanwhile, to relieve him of many of the lesser details which ate into his time and consumed his energy. The partial news vacuum was finally ended January 19 when Mr. Eisenhower, after exactly 24 weeks, resumed his regular news conferences in Washington. This conference, in the course of which he replied to 21 questions in 26 minutes, drew an attendance of 290, the largest since his first such conference in Febraury 1953.

Some time earlier it had been suggested that either Sherman Adams, Mr. Eisenhower's immediate assistant, or Vice President Richard Nixon make himself available for occasional if not periodic news conferences. As sort of first deputy to Mr. Eisenhower the former New Hampshire governor is not only fully conversant with what goes on at the top administration level but knows the President's mind and can speak with even more authority than Secretary Hagerty. The same sort of argument runs for the Vice President, who sits with the cabinet and with the National Security Council and has carried out major special assignments for the President. He is, moreover, the constitutional heir-apparent.

Another suggestion advanced was that until the President was able to resume at least occasional news conferences the correspondents be permitted to submit written questions to him through Secretary Hagerty. This would have the advantage, so the argument ran, at least of having a more direct approach to the President himself and of getting specific answers from him—assuming that he would be willing to enter into such an arrangement. But at best it would still be an impersonal and indirect contact and far less satisfactory than the normal flesh and blood relationship. It is well remembered also how unsatisfactory—and unproductive—the written question technique proved during the Harding and Coolidge administrations. Questions can always be ignored or simply brushed off with a "No comment" response.

Yet so astute a commentator as Walter Lippmann has suggested that written questions be made a permanent part of the presidential news conferences after Mr. Eisenhower's resumption of them. He made the point that even before the President's illness oral questions and answers were "not sufficiently informing—especially on intricate matters" and needed to be supplemented by written queries to which "deliberate and fully informed answers" could be made.[10]

Roscoe Drummond, of the New York *Herald Tribune,* called attention to the fact that in mid-December it had been more than four months since the President had last met the press to answer questions. In his thinking the freeing of Mr. Eisenhower from the strain of news conferences was fully justified. But he was of the opinion also that the long absence of direct contact between the President and the news men had made for "a dangerous vacuum" harmful alike to the President, the public and the government itself. He suggested that Presidential Assistant Adams hold weekly news conferences until such time as Mr. Eisenhower was equal to them or, as an alternative, that Secretary Hagerty accept written questions for the President to answer.[11]

A somewhat different point of view was held by David Lawrence, the veteran Washington writer and columnist. He was convinced that "the press conference is the biggest single strain Mr. Eisenhower has borne during his term of office." In his opinion if the issue is ever raised the public is not likely to support the idea that a President has to subject himself to such cross-examination and needling. He agreed with Lippmann that written queries would serve the purpose better and prepared answers could be given that would prevent some impromptu response that might undo months of diplomatic effort.[12]

While it is true that in the early months of his term Mr. Eisenhower

occasionally showed some signs of tension at his news conferences
this was not apparent later. He doubtless felt that he had to be on
his guard, yet for the most part he was surprisingly at ease with the
correspondents and adjusted himself readily to the give-and-take of
the conferences. It is arguable whether the contention of so able and
experienced a commentator as Lawrence is correct that the news conference is "the biggest single strain" Mr. Eisenhower has experienced
during his stay in the White House. After all, it is the President himself who makes the ground rules, who may alter them at any time,
who may decline to answer a question, who may terminate the conferences at will, and even decide whether to hold any.

As for written queries submitted in advance, there are times when
even if the President is functioning normally they might serve a useful purpose in providing detailed information as to a particular situation. During the later stages of Mr. Eisenhower's convalescence they
would have helped to supplement the flow of information from Secretary Hagerty and his staff. But in no case would they be a satisfactory substitute for the standard news conference with the President
there in the flesh to answer questions from the floor. The Eisenhower
showing in this respect prior to his illness was highly gratifying and
earned for him the respect and gratitude of the correspondents.

The simple and inescapable fact is that there is now no adequate
or acceptable substitute for the Presidential news conference as it developed from March 1933 to the summer of 1955. That it is extra-
legal and is not required of the President is relatively immaterial.
Prior to 1933 the United States was still largely insular in its outlook.
Two decades later after a global war, the Korean "police action," and
the cold war the situation was vastly different. Even ordinary communications were global in scope and practically instantaneous in terms
of speed. The American public had become accustomed, moreover,
to split-second visual news along with the printed word. Dwight D.
Eisenhower, in particular, enjoyed the confidence of the free world
and the respect even of the Communist countries to a degree unequaled
by any of his predecessors. All of this made the partial vacuum of
news from the White House in the late months of 1955 into early 1956
more important than it would have been with a lesser man involved
or had the world situation been less critical.

VII

EISENHOWER: THIRD PHASE

During his eight years in the White House, Dwight D. Eisenhower held far fewer news conferences than either of his predecessors. This was accounted for in several ways. His three major illnesses took him out of circulation for comparatively long periods and necessarily shut him off from direct contact with the news media. On his numerous trips abroad he was always accompanied by a substantial number of correspondents, but these trips meant an interruption of his normal news conferences, infrequent though they were. And in reply to a question at one of his regular news conferences in 1960 he admitted that if he had had his say in a recent fireside telecast, or in some other way, no news conference was held; in a word, the Presidential news conference depended largely upon his whim or judgment.

The news conference tally for Franklin D. Roosevelt, Truman and Eisenhower was as shown in the table below.

As these figures show, Eisenhower news conferences were held only a little more than half as often as those of Truman and not quite a third as often as those of Franklin Roosevelt.

By years, the Eisenhower news conferences were held as follows:

1953	23	1958	20
1954	33	1959	31
1955	19	1960	14
1956	24	1961	1
1957	25		

PRESIDENTIAL PRESS CONFERENCES

	Number	Months in Office	Average Yearly
Roosevelt	998	147	81.48
Truman	324	93	41.76
Eisenhower	190*	96	23.75

*A discrepancy exists as to the number of Eisenhower news conferences. The figure used here is based on a letter from Press Secretary Hagerty to the writer of May 6, 1960. Richard Friedman, in *Editor & Publisher*, Jan. 14, 1961, p. 14, gave the number up to then as 191. With the final one on January 18, the total would be 192. But both the New York *Times* and *Herald Tribune* gave the final number as 193.

In terms of the number of such conferences, Eisenhower's best years were 1954, his second in office, and 1959, his next to last full year. In the former he held 33 news conferences and in the latter 31. His two leanest years were 1955, the year of his first heart attack, and 1960. In the former he held only 19 conferences and in the latter only 14.

Perhaps from the standpoint of the news it did not make, as well as what it produced, the Eisenhower news conference of May 11, 1960 was one of his most important. On that occasion he began with some remarks about the U-2 reconnaissance flights over Russia which, in a few days, were to wreck the impending "summit" conference in Paris. The President, having made his general statement, emphasized that he would have no more to say on the subject. In the face of this, however, the correspondents were persistent and ingenious enough to pose nearly a dozen related questions, including one dealing with U.S. espionage. They had little to show for their pains.

In his opening remarks, the President stressed "the need for intelligence gathering activities," explained the nature of such activities, discussed "How should we view all this activity?" and asserted finally that "we must not be distracted from the real issues of the day by what is an accident or a symptom of the world situation." [1]

This particular news conference produced one of Mr. Eisenhower's not unrare shows of temper. He was asked to comment on a recent article by former President Truman in *Look* magazine, entitled "The Day Ike Snubbed Me." Queried about this, the President snapped, "I just haven't the time," and, his face reddening, turned quickly to another questioner. As Ed Koterba, Scripps-Howard writer, phrased it in his column a day or two later: "One must actually be present in the room to appreciate this vivid fourth dimension—the inner manifestation when the President blows his stack." [2]

Still another byproduct of this particular news conference was a revealing comment on a question as to his newspaper reading habits and how he felt about unfriendly newspaper cartoons or columns. Surprisingly he said he normally read only the Sunday papers.

"Well, I don't know whether you can call it a habit," he explained, "for the simple reason it takes a lot of time if I was going to keep track of all you people say. I take the, what I call the important sections of the Sunday papers that review world events go over the things, and those are the things I study carefully. The kind of things you talk of, cartoons and unfriendly quips, I just can't be bothered with." [3]

(By contrast, President Kennedy in his first news conference, January 25, 1961, disclosed that he read daily the Washington newspapers, the Baltimore *Sun,* the New York *Times,* the New York *Herald Tribune* and the *Wall Street Journal.*)

In his televised farewell address to the nation a few days before leaving office, Mr. Eisenhower took a moment to voice his "gratitude to the radio and television networks for the opportunities they have given me over the years to bring reports and messages to our nation." He made no mention of the fact that as against the relatively infrequent telecasts the daily newspapers and wire services had rendered this service daily during his eight years in the White House. *Editor & Publisher* wondered editorially whether this "was an inadvertent omission or a deliberate slight." Whatever the President's reasons "for ignoring the newspaper press in this comment," the periodical went on, he "should know that his fame as a general in World War II, which paved the way to the White House, was achieved mainly through the printed word—newspaper reporting and comment. And this was before television arrived on the scene." [4]

What is more, it pointed out, the time given by radio and television was contributed as a public service and not as a favor to the President. The newspaper press, it added, expected no thanks from "the President or anyone else for doing its job. But when thanks are being passed around we would think the President would have remembered that the reporters were always by his side 'to bring his reports and messages to the nation' even when the cameras and microphones couldn't be there." Conceivably the President might have added a word in his farewell address about the press, but it is doubtful if there was anything studied in the omission.

Another kind of appraisal of Mr. Eisenhower was made in the same issue by the *Editor & Publisher* Washington staff on its "Washington News Frontier" page. The consensus here was that the President had "departed from our midst neither liked nor disliked—but pretty much unknown." [5] It was commented upon that he tended to refer to reporters at his news conferences as "you people," but no offense was taken at this since he referred similarly to members of the Senate and the House as "those people."

But unlike the Truman and Franklin D. Roosevelt days the little semi-intimacies, such as Sunday evening suppers with a chosen few reporters or Saturday afternoon Potomac River "poker cruises" with still fewer, were gone. About a year before the close of the Eisenhower administration, it was noted that the President had "relaxed" by having three or four black-tie dinners for newsmen with a dozen correspondents at each. But by then, the *Editor & Publisher* staff writers pointed out, "it was kind of late in the game."

Also shortly before leaving office, they recalled, the President had a half dozen correspondents, including Arthur Krock of the New York *Times,* in for a dinner. One of the topics discussed was "what happened" in the 1960 election. Then on January 16, 1961 the President had a stag dinner for about 70 of the "regulars" who had covered the White House during his administrations. But it was noted, too, that the Eisenhowers had cancelled the annual White House formal reception for correspondents and their wives, although occasionally the head of a news association and his wife were invited to state dinners.

A footnote to all this was added by John P. O'Donnell, former head of the Washington bureau of the New York *Daily News,* who went on extended sick leave about the time Mr. Eisenhower made his exit. O'Donnell had capsule comments on Eisenhower, Truman and Franklin Roosevelt. On Eisenhower, "A lucky general." On Truman, "An amusing cuss who always realized his limitations." On Roosevelt, "too ambitious—too selfish and self-centered." [6] It was O'Donnell to whom Roosevelt pointedly gave a German Iron Cross right after a White House news conference just before the U.S. got actively into World War II.

Mr. Eisenhower held his final news conference January 18, 1961. This was the morning after his televised farewell talk to the nation and two days before he was to turn over his office to his successor. It was also his only news conference of 1961 and his first since September 7, 1960, a span of 133 days. During 1960, as noted, he held only 14 news conferences, an average of a little more than one a month. Actually, however, even this record was spotty with two in January, three in February, two in March, one each in April, May and July, none in June, three in August, one early in September and none in October, November or December. News conferences scheduled for the week of May 31 and for December 12 were called off. At least in part Mr. Eisenhower's rather frequent absences from Washington and the campaign accounted for this irregularity.

The original Eisenhower news conference on February 17, 1953 had an attendance of some 250 correspondents. The attendance at his final news conference was 309. In the intervening eight years he had adhered pretty well, through Secretary Hagerty, to his policy of permitting direct quotations and of allowing the conferences to be taped for later television release. The use of direct quotes and release of the televised film, both of which were departures from the pattern of the news conferences during earlier administrations, were subject to the final approval of Secretary Hagerty but this was always given.

On the whole, the outgoing President ended his formal relations with the news media much as he had begun—on a cordial note. But as Robert J. Donovan, veteran New York *Herald Tribune* correspondent, reported: "In many ways the President's final press conference was typical of many of the preceding 192. There were his characteristic occasional slips of the tongue—nitrogen bomb, which he corrected by hydrogen bomb, and 'insidious penetration' when he meant 'insidious penetration,' speaking of the excessive concentration on weapons instead of ideas." '

Two other things stood out at the end. The President would not be drawn into a discussion of personalities, e.g., Mr. Kennedy or Mr. Truman, and he kept his temper in hand. Even with Sarah McClendon, of the El Paso *Times,* who had roused his ire fairly often over the years, he kept his composure. There was laughter when she rose to identify herself, but her question this time was a mild one about the budget.

Inevitably the question of his relations with the press during his eight years in the White House came up. Robert G. Spivack, of the New York *Post,* reminded him that at his initial news conference the President had said there had been some speculation that a good deal of antagonism would develop between him and the reporters over the years but Mr. Eisenhower had said that "through the war years and ever since I have found nothing but desire to dig at the truth so far as I was concerned, and be open-handed and forthright about it. That is the kind of relationship I hope we can continue." Spivack asked if Mr. Eisenhower felt "during these eight years we have continued it."

The President replied: "Well, I will say this: So far as I have known the facts I have given them responsively to every question, and where I thought the national security was involved I was honest enough to say so." Spivack persisted: "I mean, did you feel that reporters had been fair to you too, in their questions?" To this the reply was, "Well, when you come down to it, I don't see what a reporter could do much to a President, do you?" At this there was laughter, but there the matter ended.

In his opening remarks, however, Mr. Eisenhower said he had come that morning "not with any particularly brilliant ideas about the future, but I did want the opportunity to say good-by to people that I have been associated with now for eight years, mostly I think on a friendly basis [laughter], and at least it certainly has always been interesting." Then he did the unusual thing of having Jack Romagna, official White House stenographer, who had transcribed every Eisenhower news conference at home and abroad, stand up. The President said that Romagna, whom he noted most of the reporters had never seen, had "been of inestimable service to the Government and to all of you." To this there were "Shouts and applause." [8]

A little later, Ed Koterba, of United Features Syndicate, remarked to the President that "it is agreed that at times over the last eight years we at the press conferences may not have been too charitable in our questioning of you." Koterba asked whether the President would elaborate "and relate to us your feeling about your relations with the press and these press conferences in particular." In reply the President pointed out that "the other evening" he had invited some 70 "regulars" to the White House. He went on: [9]

"Now I didn't ask them whether they were critics or particular friends of mine, some of them are, they've been warm personal friends, whether they were Democrats or Republicans or Socialists—but we had a good time I think, everybody seemed to, and I think that on a personal basis it was a friendly thing. So I have never objected to penetrating and searching questions. The only thing I object to is something that tries to—it's like the beating your wife question, I don't like that, and [laughter] but I have no one that I could single out and say they have been annoying nor have I anyone to argue with."

Felix Belair Jr., New York *Times* correspondent, described the President as being "in his best form for his farewell meeting with reporters, ranging in his replies from the light to the deadly serious. Physically and mentally he seemed full of bounce. He refused to be irritated by a 'loaded' question and he declined to accept an invitation to explain the Republican defeat at the polls." [10]

Press Secretary James C. Hagerty, meanwhile, set various records for that office. He held it longer than any of his predecessors, he enjoyed the President's confidence to a remarkable degree and, in consequence, served not only as an administration spokesman on important occasions, but took part in policy-making decisions especially during the second Eisenhower term, and functioned as an "advance man" for the President on trips abroad, notably the one to Japan. The President never got there as a result of anti-American feeling which reached a peak at the time of Hagerty's arrival at the Tokyo airport where he had to be rescued.

Because he was forthright and candid, some correspondents were critical of Hagerty but they were in the minority. The majority point of view was summed up by James Marlow, Associated Press news analyst, in a column which appeared shortly before Eisenhower and Hagerty left office. "For eight years a take-charge man with big eyeglasses and more than enough chin," Marlow began, "did an extraordinary job of helping his boss, the President of the United States, over the rough spots of public relations . . . .When he turned in his resignation, Eisenhower said he had been invaluable. And indeed he was.

"Hagerty . . . was to a large extent the President's eyes and ears in the world of general news. He was more than that. He not only was a buffer between the President and the press to a degree unmatched in this century. He was also times without number Eisenhower's mouthpiece. But he was no blabbermouth. He never got his devotion to news mixed up with his loyalty to Eisenhower. He never said anything to embarrass his boss. He didn't make slips." In Marlow's view, Hagerty's success stemmed from two things which many pubilc relations men never learn: "He paid attention to details and informed himself on problems he had to handle." [11]

In an exchange of letters on January 9, the President praised Hagerty for his "understanding and intelligence" and for his "great knowledge of the technical aspects of the distribution of news which has enabled the people of the country to get the broadest and most comprehensive coverage of events that has ever been possible." Hagerty on his part, wrote that he was "extremely proud" to have served on Eisenhower's personal staff. "I only hope," he added, "that I have been able to absorb to some degree the great wisdom, forbearance and understanding that have always guided your actions as President of the United States." [12] Even his critics probably would concede that indeed he had done this.

In sum, the Eisenhower administration closed in an atmosphere of good feeling with the news media. The correspondents, on the whole, respected the outgoing President. Relations between him and them, in the main, had been cooperative and cordial although never intimate. If there was little of the easy give-and-take that marked much of the long Franklin D. Roosevelt period, Mr. Eisenhower, in contrast with his predecessor, Harry S. Truman, was generally more predictable and consistent in his dealings with the press corps. During his two terms in the White House he profited from the capable help of Press Secretary Hagerty who, as noted, attained stature as an administration spokesman and policy maker of sorts to a degree unequaled by any previous press secretary.

To the Eisenhower administration must go credit for extending the dimensions of White House news conferences by permitting television cameras to record them and by allowing practically unlimited direct quotation of the President's replies to questions. Technically both of these were still subject to White House release and approval, but the fact that these controls were not exercised during the eight Eisenhower years was more significant than the fact that they existed.

It remained for the incoming President, John F. Kennedy, to take an immediate further step forward. This was to permit live telecasting of his first two news conferences. The reaction to this was generally favorable, especially on the part of the viewing public. There was good indication that the Kennedy administration would make more vigorous use of the public relations potential of the White House news conferences, especially through live TV. But after its first two months in office there was same dissatisfaction over the very size of the Kennedy news conferences, over the resulting confusion, and over a tendency of television to hamper the news function.

VIII

THE KENNEDY YEARS

For more than 150 years the Presidents of the United States have had their troubles with the American press, and vice versa. From Washington through John F. Kennedy the story has been much the same but with marked individual differences. The basic problem has been two-fold: First, how can the President and his administration get their best image across to the American public? Second, and more importantly, how can the news media get and convey to that public all of the news, information and opinion they must have so as to inform the public promptly and adequately?

It is 50 years since Woodrow Wilson undertook to hold the first formal and regular White House news conferences. His limited experience with them was unhappy and the experiment soon ended. The conferences were resumed by Warren G. Harding, were continued routinely under Calvin Coolidge, fell off under Herbert Hoover, reached a new peak under Franklin D. Roosevelt, and were useful and fruitful under Harry S. Truman and Dwight D. Eisenhower.

The second Roosevelt gave the news conferences new dimensions. Further changes were made during the Truman and Eisenhower periods. One was to permit direct quotations at news conferences. Another was to let television cameras tape the news conferences for broadcast later. Both developments brought the President into closer touch with the public.

Still more changes occurred in the thirty-four months under President Kennedy. These arose from the nature of the man, from events, from changes in policy, and from expanded and improved communications facilities. If anything, Mr. Kennedy was more continuously in the public eye than either of his immediate predecessors. Some changes or innovations affecting White House relations with the news media during his brief administration were:

1. Live telecasts and broadcasts of Presidential news conferences.

2. Rather frequent exclusive interviews with various reporters and writers.

3. Unusual intimacy with certain correspondents, including swimming in the White House pool, or as a dinner guest in their homes.

4. Luncheons with groups of newspapermen—editors and publishers

—by individual states to discuss mutual problems and matters of public concern.

5. A shift in the scheduling of news conferences mostly to afternoons so that no morning session was held between March 31 and the final one on November 14, 1963.

More than any other President except Theodore Roosevelt, John F. Kennedy was a recognized writer in his own right. Both he and Mrs. Kennedy, by a coincidence, had been in newspaper work before they entered public life. As a reporter for International News Service, the future President in 1945 covered the organization of the United Nations in San Francisco, the victory of the Labor Party in Great Britain, and the Potsdam Conference. Mrs. Kennedy had worked as an inquiring photographer for the then Washington *Times-Herald*. Not long after that she met Mr. Kennedy, then a young Congressman. Richard M. Nixon, destined to be Mr. Kennedy's opponent in the 1960 Presidential election, was said to have been the first man she interviewed.

The Kennedy exposure to active newspaper work was of limited duration, but he earned a solid place for himself as a serious writer. As a comparatively young man, he wrote a book, *Why England Slept,* which was an account of that nation's appeasement of Hitler and its consequences. While he was recovering later from major surgery on his back, he wrote *Profiles in Courage.* This won for him in 1957 a Pulitzer Prize for biography. In his pre-Presidential days he also wrote magazine articles.

Out of this varied and rather substantial experience he might have been forgiven or at least understood if, as President, he sometimes reminded reporters that he once had been one of them and knew something about the craft of writing. But there is no record, at least at his news conferences, that he ever did.

Less than a month after the start of the Kennedy administration, questions were being raised as to some of its news practices and policies. *Editor & Publisher,* the principal trade publication, in an editorial in its February 4, 1961, issue, listed seven instances in the handling of information by government officials in such a way, in its thinking, as to constitute a "disturbing trend."[1] This was followed shortly by an exchange of letters on the subject between Eugene S. Pulliam, Jr., of the Indianapolis *News,* as chairman of the American Society of Newspaper Editors freedom of information committee, and Presidential Press Secretary Pierre Salinger. Pulliam wrote on February 15 but Salinger did not reply until April 18, the eve of the ASNE meeting.

Two features of that meeting were a brief informal talk by the President on April 20 and a panel discussion that morning on the administration's public information policies. Because of the recency of the Bay of Pigs business, Mr. Kennedy scrapped the formal talk he had prepared. The situation in Cuba, he reported briefly, was "worse" rather than better. But he reminded the ASNE members, "There are from this sobering lesson useful lessons for us all to learn." He was annoyed by advance stories on the impending invasion intended to free Cuba from Castro.[2]

At the morning session sparks flew when Secretary Salinger defended the administration's news policies. Peter Lisagor, of the Chicago *Daily News,* insisted that more could be accomplished if the President talked with five reporters instead of 400. Salinger retorted that he would be happy to let Lisagor select five from the 1,000 then accredited. He added that the news conferences would be more fruitful if the reporters improved their questions. He challenged them to forget "the pet questions their editors have given them to ask."

At the ANPA Bureau of Advertising dinner in New York City just a week later, the President spoke at some length on the dilemma of full information of government activities without violating national security. He referred to the "clear and present danger" arising out of the current Cuban situation. He rejected any idea of official censorship, and insisted that he had no thought of setting up another Office of War Information.

Specifically, he declared that the challenge of the times "imposes upon our society two requirements of direct concern to both press and the President—two requirements that may seem almost contradictory in tone, but which must be reconciled and fulfilled if we are to meet this national peril. I refer, first, to the need for greater public information; and second, to the need for far greater secrecy . . ."

He warned at the same time that no administration official, "high or low, civilian or military, should interpret my words here tonight as an excuse to censor the news, to stifle dissent, to cover up our mistakes or to withhold from the press and the public the facts they deserve to know."

At the same time, he asked "every publisher, every editor and every newsman in the nation to reexamine his own standards, and to recognize the nature of our country's peril." Even the protection of the First Amendment, he asserted, "must yield to the public's need for national security." To the question, "is it news?" he contended every newspaper must now ask itself about every story, "Is it in the national interest?" [3]

He then offered to cooperate "wholeheartedly" with any recommendations as to "the voluntary assumption of specific new steps or machinery" the newspaper industry might suggest. Newspaper editors agreed generally as to the need for press responsibility and self-restraint. But many of them wanted Mr. Kennedy to be more specific.

Felix H. McKnight, of the Dallas *Times Herald,* president of the ASNE, and Mark Ferree, of Scripps-Howard, president of the ANPA, asked the President to set up a meeting for a discussion of these common problems. Mr. Kennedy chose May 9, 1961. Others representing the industry on that unique occasion were the presidents of the Associated Press and United Press International, and two directors each from the ASNE and the ANPA. It was an odd coincidence that McKnight, as executive editor of his paper, was to take personal charge of its news operations on the afternoon the President was assassinated in Dallas 29 months later.

The meeting with the President was friendly enough. The conferees explored various aspects of the news vs. security problems involved. In the end no definite agreement was reached except to schedule another such conference. No date was set and, as it turned out, it was never to be held.

But in December 1962, newspaper organization representatives met and discussed Mr. Kennedy's original attitude as to government news dissemination. This was two months after the U.S.-Soviet confrontation over Russian missiles in Cuba. At that time the White House had asked the U.S. press to observe a security guidelist of "sensitive areas" of information. This list was much like the restrictions in the voluntary censorship code which was in force during World War II.

Out of the December 1962 meeting came a statement on news and security which said in part: [4]

"We are concerned lest government go beyond the legitimate suppression of strictly military information and look upon news of what the government is doing not as an honest report of what has happened, but as a means to some desired end ...

"The security of the nation can be maintained only by the full reporting of all the truth that is not harmful to the national military interest."

President Kennedy showed his personal interest in the press in various ways. One was his concern over the prolonged newspaper strikes in New York, Cleveland and elsewhere. In the New York situation he went so far as to criticize the tactics of Bert Powers, leader of the International Typographical Union strikers. He offered the help of Labor Secretary Willard Wirtz in settling the dispute although he did not regard it as something to be settled by government interference.

At his May 9, 1962, news conference he was asked how he felt about the press generally, "as you see it from the Presidency . . . its treatment of your Administration, its treatment of the issues of the day." His reply was both frank and revealing. He said:

"Well, I am reading more and enjoying it less, and so on, but I have not complained nor do I plan to make any general complaints. I read and talk to myself about it, but I don't plan to issue any general statement on the press.

"I think they are doing their task, as a critical branch, the fourth estate. And I am attempting to do mine. And we are going to live together for a period, and then go our separate ways."

But this was not to be.

Questions at various news conferences elicited from Mr. Kennedy his ideas or opinions about his dealings with the news media people. Less than a month after his inauguration, at his February 8, 1961, news conference, he was asked about the "wide open news conference" as opposed to the practice of government officials not identifying themselves in news briefings. His reply was, "Well, they are hazardous in many cases . . ." Queried as to whether the press abused him somewhat, he answered, "Well, you subject me to some abuse, but not to any lack of respect." [5]

Mr. Kennedy was definitely quicker and far more articulate in his responses to news conference questioners than his predecessor had been. But there were times when even he seemed to fumble for words. For example, the frequency of news conferences had fallen off in the autumn of 1961. At his November 8, 1961, news conference a questioner asked whether the reporters could do anything to encourage more frequent meetings with him. "Well, I like them," he replied, "But —sort of—but I will—let me say that I'll hold these—I'm anxious to hold press conferences as often as I believe it to be in the public interest." [6]

At a later news conference he was asked directly whether he favored major government stories going to a limited number of reporters who might be called in or whether, as a matter of policy, he would advise his administration that the news should flow freely to all reporters equally. His reply was fairly specific: "I think—yes, I will let them know, and I think it ought to . . . I don't think there should

be a discrimination because of size or sex or any other reason."[7] But
in the months that followed the administration practice was sometimes
quite the opposite.

One of the final acts of President Kennedy's public life was his
appearance November 18, 1963, before the Inter-American Press
Association in Miami Beach. In his address he pointed out that two
of the guests, once high Peruvian officials, were now newspaper publishers. "It does suggest to those who hold office," he remarked, "that
when the time comes that if, as they say in the United States, if you
can't beat them, join them."[8] Four days later he was dead.

Despite the greater exposure of the Kennedy administration to the
reporters, this did not lessen its difficulties with them nor diminish the
criticism. Much of this doubtless would have occurred under any
administration. Some of it was the result of the sensitive and even
dangerous developments like the Cuban crisis of October 1962 and the
worsening situation in South Vietnam in the fall of 1963.

A major criticism centered in the administration's policies on "managed" news. Part of this stemmed from an administrative effort to
achieve a measure of unity in its news policies. There was good reason
for this to a point. There was trouble when the Defense Department,
for example, said one thing, the State Department had another version, and the White House had to extricate itself from the resulting
difficulty.

At times administration spokesmen compounded the trouble. One
of the worst of these occurred when Assistant Secretary of Defense
(for Public Affairs) Arthur Sylvester first defended managed news
as "part of the arsenal of weaponry that a President has." A few days
later in justifying his stand he asserted that it was "the government's
inherent right to lie, if necessary" in a major crisis.[9] As a former, longtime newsman he should have known that such an utterance would
cause loud outcries. Walter Lippmann said Sylvester violated the first
principle of managed news, which is "never to admit it."

On a lesser scale was Operation Big Lift in October 1963, which
made West Germany and other NATO nations apprehensive that by
dramatically flying an armored division to Germany the United States
was really getting ready to reduce its combat forces there. This was
confirmed partly by an Assistant Secretary of Defense, not Sylvester,
but President Kennedy flatly denied any such intention at his October
31, 1963, news conference.

Press Secretary Salinger was thoroughly sold on the "live" news
conferences via radio and television; in fact, the idea was credited to

him. But not everyone was happy with the arrangement. Peter Lisagor, of the Chicago *Daily News*, described them as "a mess . . . disorderly, disorganized, almost chaotic." As for the correspondents who attended them, Lisagor called them "little more than props in a show."

The Kennedy news conference protocol, carried over from previous administrations, held firm. A session opened with any formal announcement Mr. Kennedy had to make, followed by recognition of the senior Associated Press or United Press International correspondent. Others were then called upon as—and if—they caught the President's eye. The conferences still ran exactly 30 minutes and ended automatically when the senior news service reporter said, "Thank you, Mr. President."

Despite the usefulness of the revised format, with live television, there were strong criticisms of the way it operated. One was that too many reporters tended to make speeches or to ask multiple questions. This limited the number of questioners and often prevented the President from answering in depth. Another criticism was that certain correspondents tended to "ham it up," thus cheapening the conference.

One corrective suggestion was to go back to the practice of written questions, submitted in advance, as was done under Coolidge. But that sorry experience was one deterrent. Another strong argument against this was that it would put even more power in the hands of the President to shape news or, worse, to suppress it. In any case Mr. Kennedy was on record at one of his news conferences as not desiring to change their format.

The charge that the Kennedy administration sought to "manage" the news was unquestionably true in degree. Such a policy from its viewpoint was understandable. It had ample historical precedent since nearly every President, from Washington through Eisenhower, at one time or other and in one way or other, sought to manipulate the news and control it to a degree. It has even been said that George Washington's summoning of David Claypoole, of the *Pennsylvania Packet and Daily Advertiser*, about publishing his Farewell Address was in fact a kind of management of the news to get the best effect.

To be fair, the recent issue was partly one of semantics. Correspondent May Craig at a news conference in February 1963 asked the President to define "managed news" and to tell "why you find it necessary to practice it." The President replied in part that "we have had very limited success in managing the news, if that is what we

have been trying to do." Even newspapermen conceded that the
press itself "manages" the news in a sense. What was more important,
therefore, than whether the news was being "managed"—that is,
shaped or directed or, worse, restricted—was the dual question of who
was trying to "manage" the news and, especially, to what end?

In the recent White House news operation not only was President
Kennedy of a different mold from former President Eisenhower, but
Press Secretary Salinger was quite different from James C. Hagerty,
his predecessor. Salinger was younger, more gregarious and generally
more affable than Hagerty, although both have tempers. There were
marked differences also in their methods of operation.

An autographed photograph of President Kennedy in Salinger's
office was inscribed "To Pierre Salinger—the voice of the White
House." The description was substantially true but was only partly
accurate. Salinger himself emphasized that the administration had
"attempted to open up the White House . . . so that reporters go
around and see members of the staff without having to check with"
his office. As a result, to quote further, "they feel freedom around
the White House in talking to people and developing their own stories."
For perhaps the first time they had frequent and direct access to Presidential advisers. But there was testimony that at times this was
at the price of stricter control of "hard" news.[10]

The consensus of White House correspondents was that there was
greater access to prime sources. One veteran reporter said, "There's
more individual access to the President now than before . . . This individual accessibility is great. It is not a leak system or a system
of palace favorites . . . It's often to the Administration's advantage
to see a reporter and help him on a story and make sure that the public is accurately informed."

Under Mr. Kennedy it was generally agreed that Salinger was successful in handling White House press relations. But in May 1963
Salinger himself remarked, "I've often said that John F. Kennedy is
his own best press secretary." In large measure this was true.

Like previous press secretaries, Salinger had his critics, both mild
and otherwise. A friendly correspondent remarked that "He gets
sloppy sometimes and gives the wrong facts. They're mostly minor
but they can become quite important . . . He lies a little too much.
Some of that's necessary, but he carries it too far." A reporter for a
Washington daily agreed that "Salinger has told lies to reporters, including me. But that was a couple of years ago, and I think he's
learned his lesson."

Yet a television network correspondent felt that while Salinger had "always been honest," on occasion "he had to fudge to cover up things." *Life* magazine pointed out that he was "quick to admit his mistakes, which happen more over small matters than large ones." [11] One "slip" at a White House briefing which, as Salinger admitted, annoyed the President was an erroneous report that all White House servants had promised in writing not to write stories of their association with the Kennedys.

In a comparison of his role in the Kennedy administration with that of Hagerty previously, Salinger called his predecessor "active in the formulation of foreign and domestic policy." But he remarked that "I have more influence in the formulation of information policy and there is more coordination." [Management?] Where Hagerty had to interpret the press for Mr. Eisenhower, Salinger worked for a President who, as noted, had been a working newspaperman himself briefly.

A byproduct of this awareness, in the words of another White House correspondent, not only was that Mr. Kennedy "reads every damn thing written" but "his skin is as thin as cigarette paper." This sensitivity was reflected in the cancellation for a time of the 22 White House subscriptions to the New York *Herald Tribune*, which had given offense.

From long exposure President Kennedy, as the *U.S. News & World Report* once observed, not only had many friends in the press corps but "uses them to get across his story, often on the basis of exclusive information fed to them." When complaints were made about this practice, Mr. Kennedy told a news conference not only was he going "to keep my old friends," but the Presidency was not "a good place to make" new ones.

In Salinger's view there was nothing wrong with such a method of disseminating news. Early in the administration *Editor & Publisher* quoted him as saying, "I see no requirement that just became one guy gets it everybody gets it. Mr. Kennedy has had innumerable private talks with newsmen. Sometimes stories are written from these talks without showing that they talked with the President, . . ." [12] Hugh Sidey, of *Time* magazine and a Kennedy biographer, noted that Mr. Kennedy considered "himself a better PR man than anyone around him and this erodes the press secretary's job." Another correspondent called the President "his own best press secretary" and in his view Salinger was doing the job the way the President wanted it done.

But a third reporter described Salinger's office as the "most inefficient in history, never on time with anything and hardly any concern with other people's deadlines, . . ." Yet he conceded that it was "great on substance. I think I'd rather have substance than efficiency. It comes in the work they'll do for you when approached. They'll help you on a story by getting you in to the President or seeing him for you."

A 1963 poll of leading Washington correspondents by *Newsweek* magazine was revealing in this respect. Twenty-eight believed that Hagerty was fairer and more competent than Salinger. But reporters felt much more warmly toward Salinger "than they did to Hagerty. He can be frank, tough, witty, and perhaps more important thick skinned." In sum, Salinger was regarded as "enormously popular" if not always as accurate or as well informed as he should be.[13]

The Salinger influence was felt in another direction. This had to do with press officers in other major government departments. Not only were policy statements from them cleared first with Salinger, but he was influential as to who were named to these posts. This was part of the administration policy of coordinating information. This had advantages, but it also obviously had a bearing on the cry of "managed" news.

It was also in line with the first of seven basic information rules laid down by the President: more centralization of information on foreign and military policy and basic domestic policy. The second Kennedy requirement, that the military must be kept firmly in line under civilians, was successful to a degree.[14] But it also was criticized because, it was argued, it shut off dissent, especially on the part of high ranking military officers such as the joint chiefs of staff.

In times of crisis it is hard to draw the line between what is to be reported and what is not. This was illustrated sharply during the October 1962 Cuban crisis. As Clark Mollenhoff, 1961 Pulitzer Prize winner for Washington reporting, put it: "For a period of several days in late October, our knowledge and our coverage were largely limited to the facts that were fed us through the Pentagon, the State Department, and the White House. There was no power to go behind the self-serving declaration of the Kennedy administration, and for the time being most of us were willing to put up with it."[15]

Merriman Smith, veteran White House correspondent, was another who objected to the restrictions and was critical of Presidential advisers who believed that the press should "report with onesided fairness." To him they were "pseudo-saviors who think the press is a large, inanimate gramophone to be cut on and off at the will of the government." He excluded Salinger from any such group.[16]

In March 1963 Salinger defended the restrictions on news during the Cuban crisis. "We did not lie to the American people," he asserted. "We did not deprive the American people of any information except that which, for the highest national security, had to be withheld from our adversaries." He countered with the argument that the only "legitimate place" where news could be "managed" was on editorial desks. He suggested that a "really fundamental study" was needed there to find out whether news was being "managed" in the public interest.[17]

Significantly, former Secretary Hagerty, in the *National Observer*, declared that "If there is managed news, then it's the responsibility of the press, not the Government." [18]

As in the Eisenhower administration, the frequency of news conferences held by President Kennedy was variable. In 1961 Mr. Kennedy held 19, in 1962 had 27, and in 1963 there were 17, including one at Bonn, Germany, and one with business editors.[19] The total was 63 in 34 months, or slightly fewer relatively than for Mr. Eisenhower in a similar span. Mr. Kennedy was away from Washington more than his predecessor—215 days as against 195 for Mr. Eisenhower in an equivalent period.

Another difference between the two administrations lay in their handling of Presidential ailments. When Mr. Eisenhower was stricken in the summer of 1955, the news was given out promptly and in precise detail and Secretary Hagerty continued this practice. The same was true of the later Eisenhower illnesses.

It was well known when Mr. Kennedy took office that he had back problems resulting from his World War II injury. But when the President reinjured his back at a ceremonial tree planting in Canada the fact was suppressed and only came to light later. The Kennedy rocking chair figured in this, and for a time the President was on crutches. The incident was significant only for contrast and by fears on the part of some correspondents that if the White House was less than frank in this matter, it might be so in others.

Despite the claims of the Kennedy administration that the doors of government were more open to reporters, there was evidence that they were sometimes open to the favored few or at what seemed a price. At the same time there were restrictions, as in the case of the Nevada nuclear tests or harassment and intimidation over Pentagon news by Federal Bureau of Investigation agents which in some respects tended to offset the gains made in the free flow of information.

Deterioration in the administration's relations with the news media and the resultant dangers inherent in this situation were pinpointed by two highly respected commentators, Arthur Krock and Hanson W. Baldwin, both of the New York *Times*. The Krock article, "Mr. Kennedy's Management of the News," in the March 1963 issue of *Fortune* magazine, was reprinted in the *Congressional Record—Appendix* of February 26, 1963. That by Baldwin, "Managed News: Our Peacetime Censorship," in the April 1963 *Atlantic Monthly*, was reprinted similarly in the April 24, 1963, *Congressional Record—Appendix.*[20]

The criticism of these two veteran and highly regarded writers ran in similar vein. Krock believed that under Mr. Kennedy a policy of news management existed not only "in the form of direct and deliberate action," but was "enforced more cynically and boldly than by any previous administration" at a time when the U.S. was not at war nor threatened with war. "In the form of indirect but equally deliberate action," he added, "the policy has been much more effective than direct action in coloring the several facets of public information, because it has been employed with subtlety and imagination for which there is no historic parallel known to me." (Krock has been identified with the Washington scene since the Taft administration.)

Apart from national matters, Krock defined government management of news as consisting "of attempts by any official unit or individual in an area of authority to influence the presentation of the news." Ways of doing this, he added, are by "suppression, concealment, distortion, and false weighting of the facts to which the public is entitled." It can be achieved also through the use of threats or implied threats, or by closing legitimate sources of information to writers who have gotten facts whose publication would embarrass government "for personal, policy, or political reasons." Another method is by giving information off the record only which makes the reporter responsible and makes it possible to disavow it when it proves inexpedient.

Indirect news management has much the same aim as direct control but is broader in scope. A major form in the Kennedy era, in Krock's opinion, "is social flattery of Washington reporters and columnists—many more than ever got this treatment in the past—by the President and his high level subordinates." Counter to this, Krock charged Mr. Kennedy with "bristling sensitiveness to critical analysis" that has not been exceeded "by any previous occupant of the White

House." One form of flattery took shape in exclusive interviews or briefings in which Mr. Kennedy went far beyond either Mr. Truman or Mr. Eisenhower. Against this, in turn, was the administration's use of the FBI and alleged wire-tapping to run down the sources of certain news stories, especially out of the Pentagon.

In line with this was a directive to subordinates by Assistant Defense Secretary Sylvester that correspondents' requests for legitimate news or for help in evaluating it could be met in only one of two ways: an official could discuss it only if a colleague was present, or by apprising Sylvester's office promptly as to the topic discussed. The natural result, Krock observed, was "sharply to reduce the transmission to the American people of objective and informed analysis of actions in foreign policy and international situations to which these actions were addressed."

Managed leaks were another form of control. These were not invented by the Kennedy administration but perhaps were being used more than ever. A Washington reporter of nearly 50 years' experience there told this writer of being the recipient of such a leak about the impending coup in South Vietnam a week or 10 days before it actually occurred in the fall of 1963. This device can be useful but it can also be dangerous and discriminatory if abused.

Another criticism was over the issuing of partial or, as it turned out, misleading statements on matters of importance. This again was not new with the Kennedy administration. One such announcement, made at an hour inconvenient for most correspondents, had to do with the investigation into excessive government stockpiling of raw materials. Another concerned oil imports. An instance of withholding involved a study by the Brookings Institution, at taxpayers' expense, of the balance-of-payments problem.

In Krock's view, the management of news in the Kennedy period was chiefly by indirect methods. As he summarized it, "This is a public relations project and the President is its most brilliant operator. Since the immediate objectives of this selling job are the news reporters in general . . ., widely read commentators and flattered editors, publishers and network moguls in particular, the project is much more accurately identified as 'managing the purveyors of the news.'" For whatever success the project had, Krock asserted, "the principal onus rests on the printed and electronic press itself."

Baldwin, on his part, remarked that the issue of squaring security with freedom was an old one. It has troubled many administrations but "national security" recently had been used, in his opinion, as an

excuse to suppress or withhold information from the public through the
news media when a) no security was actually involved or b) Russia or
other possible enemies already knew more about it than the American
public. Wartime restrictions, in fact, have not only been maintained
but, in some instances, their use has been extended on flimsy grounds.
As Baldwin saw it the push for nearly 20 years had been clearly toward greater secrecy.

Like Krock, Baldwin conceded that Mr. Kennedy in his news conferences and otherwise had been "articulate, winning and persuasive."
But he noted also that Mr. Kennedy and those about him had been
highly "sensitive to the image of the man and the office" as reflected
by the communications media. In Baldwin's view there was a prime
question as to the methods used in the government's public relations
policies and doubt whether the public was really sharing the confidence
of the President as it had in World War II and Korea. In support
of this view Baldwin cited examples similar to those presented by
Krock and others.

Baldwin also cited the carefully released background information
sometimes given, without attribution, by the President or by some
other high official. He charged that this means had been used to weak-
en the positions of such public figures as Chester Bowles, Gen. Lyman
N. Lemnitzer, and even Ambassador Adlai Stevenson. Baldwin saw
the policy of the "open door," emphasized by the Kennedy administration, as akin to "the calculated leak." It was used, he added, as an
aftermath to the Cuban crisis in a series of now-it-can-be-told articles
in leading magazines.

Baldwin referred to Sylvester as a symbol of administration policy,
noting that the latter executed it but did not set the policy. Like
others, he saw danger in the assistant defense secretary's statement
to the Associated Press that news generated by governmental action
as to content and timing was "part of the weaponry that a President
has." This was both underscored and compounded by Sylvester's
subsequent assertion as to "the government's inherent right to lie if
necessary to save itself when faced with nuclear disaster". Sylvester
added that the Pentagon would continue to use news to advance the
aims of U.S. foreign policy on the ground that "information is power."
To Louis Lyons, of the Nieman Foundation, at Harvard, this was "the
philosophy of totalitarianism." [21]

The personal approach was used in the Kennedy administration to
a degree unmatched previously. This applied to Mr. Kennedy himself, who was known to use the telephone to criticize or compliment

a reporter or editor for a story which annoyed or pleased him. After the publication in the September 1961 issue of *Fortune* magazine of a detailed account by Charles J. V. Murphy a veteran correspondent, of the Laos and Bay of Pigs failures, the President condemned the article at a news conference. Then Gen. Maxwell D. Taylor was sent to New York to see Publisher Henry Luce about the matter but got scant satisfaction.

Presidential advisers, including Attorney General Kennedy, Theodore Sorensen, and Salinger, were said to have used direct methods also in dealing with the press. Once when a Washington newspaper ran an editorial asserting that the facts it had were not wholly in accord with the President's account of the matter, Salinger was said to have phoned an executive of the paper to demand whether it was questioning the President's veracity. As Fletcher Knebel, of *Look* magazine, put it: "Never before have so few bawled out so many so often for so little." [22]

Another reporter once had a confrontation with Secretary Salinger over the exclusion of newsmen from the Nevada nuclear test site. According to him, the press secretary admitted having had something to do with the "clampdown," and was "belligerent" about his right to take such action. [23]

Whatever gains, then, were achieved by the Kennedy administration in its news relations, they were offset by certain criticisms of its news policies that were somewhat alarming and that, if persisted in, could have led to an erosion of the basic rights of the U.S. public to know. These criticisms follow:

1. The effort to "manage" the news.

2. The attempt to "unify" government news sources, as exemplified by the Defense Department directive as to clearing news and background information.

3. Suppression and distortion of the news—part of the "management" concept—as exemplified not only in the Cuban crisis but also in a number of lesser known incidents.

4. Harassment of reporters, government officials and Pentagon personnel by the FBI as to where reporters got certain news.

5. The play to White House favorites among the correspondents to the disadvantage of others and to serve the purposes of the administration.

After nearly three years under Mr. Kennedy, the Presidential news conference was more than ever a useful and necessary means of keeping the U.S. and even the world public informed. But there were

differences, some obvious, and some subtle or even obscure. On the
obvious side, to name only two, were the live broadcasting and telecasting of the conferences and the contrast between the young and
dynamic President Kennedy and the more serious, less articulate and
matter-of-fact President Eisenhower.

On the side of subtlety was the fact, as Tom Wicker, of the New
York *Times* Washington bureau, expressed it, that under Mr. Kennedy the news conference became "more an instrument of Presidential power than a useful tool of the press."²⁴ This could be because of
a second criticism, namely, that the news conference had become
too big.

But it was precisely at the point where subtlety faded into something else that the principle of the free flow of information, which
is the basic purpose of the news conference, seemed to be in some
danger. There was some threat of danger also in the "unified voice
of government" concept, however logical it seemed, coupled with large
or small falsehoods when they appeared useful, with punitive heavy-
handedness on occasion, and with too much favoritism in places where
it suited administration purposes.

The remedies for this situation, should it continue under another
administration, are several. One is for the news media to stick ever-
lastingly to their function of probing government and those who man
it. Another is to make better use of existing facilities and resources
with fewer "nit-picking" questions and less "hamming" at news conferences. Another is for those in government never to forget that
their primary responsibility is to the U.S. public and does not lie
only in mere political expediency. The historic right of the U.S.
public to know is above parties, politics and politicians.

In sum, in its nearly three years in office the Kennedy administration
in its relations with the news media and their personnel generally enjoyed a degree of warmth, accessibility and cordiality unmatched by
any previous administration. This was due in large part to the personal qualities of President Kennedy and Secretary Salinger, who set
the pace and the tone.

Weighing the pluses and minuses of the relations between the media
and Mr. Kennedy—indeed, between them and the government generally—the time seemed ripe for a reassessment of the entire relationship. Doubtless many of the criticisms by newsmen against the Kennedy administration were the result of changing times and condi-
ions. The very expansiveness of the Kennedy news conferences detracted from their effectiveness. This suggested the need for a re-

view of policies and procedures between government and the news media.

It was a significant development also that, although he did not announce his ultimate intentions, President Johnson in his first two months in office did not hold a single news conference under the Kennedy format.   Instead, he had a number of highly informal sessions with White House newsmen both there and at his Texas ranch.   At none of these were more than 60 newsmen present. Televised news conferences were not ruled out, but the signs were that Mr. Johnson preferred simpler and more direct methods which could lead to an improved and more effective relationship at least with the executive branch.

IX

"ALL THE WAY WITH L. B. J."

One of the chief slogans of the pro-Johnson wing of the Democratic party prior to and during the 1960 convention was "All the Way With L.B.J." As it turned out the nomination went to John F. Kennedy. The latter quickly offered the second spot on the ticket to his older, politically more experienced but now defeated rival from Texas. The offer was accepted.

Although as the leader of the Democratic majority in the Senate Mr. Johnson had been one of the most powerful men in Washington, as Vice President he stepped back into those political shadows reserved especially for the Number Two man in any administration. He presided over the Senate, he sat with the President in meetings of the Cabinet and the Security Council, and he represented the President on certain occasions. But if he had opinions as to how the executive branch was functioning or how certain crises, such as the Bay of Pigs fiasco or the worsening situation in South VietNam, were being handled he kept them to himself; at least, they did not become public.

Then in the twinkling of an eye, as a result of the tragic events of November 22, 1963, Mr. Johnson found himself President. The nation unpredictably had, indeed, gone "all the way with L.B.J." In place of the silent, unobtrusive Vice President, another Lyndon B. Johnson emerged, a man of surprising vigor, one who had opinions and, while choosing his words carefully, did not hesitate in stating his position at every opportunity, one who to the despair of the Secret Service showed his preference quickly for moving among the people and who perhaps, despite the recent tragic lesson, took even more chances than Mr. Kennedy. In perhaps no other area was the policy of "All the Way With L.B.J." more evident than in his unprecedented dealings with the news media and the news correspondents.

More than anything else, the first six months of Lyndon B. Johnson's tenure showed that the so-called "pattern" of the Presidential news conferences depends upon the incumbent and his wishes in such matters. In his first half year after succeeding President Kennedy, Mr. Johnson surprised the press and the public in a number of ways in his relations with the news media and the men and women representing them.

At least four differences from the previous regime in respect to the news conferences developed in that brief period: (1) the new President was more folksy than his predecessor, (2) he was more informal and formal news conferences were the exception rather than the rule as they had been under Mr. Kennedy, (3) the Johnson news conferences were much more frequent—twenty-six in the first 182 days, and (4) they were frequently given on such short notice - as little as five minutes - as to seem almost impulsive.

It was not surprising, then, that the Johnson performance in this area in those first six months produced a number of innovations. This was not to say that they were necessarily precedents. Three will illustrate this inventive trend. One was the conference at the "L.B.J." ranch, when the President spoke to the reporters from an improvised set-up on bales of hay. Another was his quick-step tour of the south grounds of the White House - seven times around - with the reporters streaming in his wake amid a running fire of conversation. The third, two days later, was the circus-like air on the White House grounds May 6 when the wives and children of correspondents came, as the President said, to see their husbands and fathers at work. Following this George Dixon, a syndicated columnist, commented that Mr. Johnson had "now held press conferences almost everywhere except in Lincoln's bed and underwater, . . ." [1]

Near the end of Mr. Johnson's first half year as President, Eric Sevareid, of the C.B.S. staff, noted in a TV commentary just after a Johnson performance that the President was following a carrot-and-stick technique in at least some of his dealings with the news media. Some basis for such an opinion apparently existed but it was open to some doubt on two counts: there was not enough evidence in so short a time to justify its being regarded as a studied policy, and in any case the President quickly found a variety of means to deal with the correspondents, with emphasis on the personal touch.

Two other developments marked the first months of the Johnson administration. One was a decided shrinkage in the number of correspondents who were able to attend the news conferences, especially on such short notice. The effect was to reduce the number of those actually present to the so-called White House "regulars," that is, those who tended to be around the White House during the working day. This caused a little grumbling since these correspondents never knew when the President might decide to hold a news conference, including such unusual hours as late in the day or especially on Saturdays. Instead of having 300 or more at a formal news conference, as in the Kennedy days, Mr. Johnson usually had fifty to sixty - more than enough for his purposes but not enough from the viewpoint of the massive Washington press corps.

Another major change, perhaps not inevitable but occurring sooner than expected, was the rather early and sudden replacement of Pierre Salinger by George Reedy as Presidential press secretary. At the outset the indications were that Salinger would retain his position indefinitely. Both President Johnson and Salinger himself had indicated this in so many words. Then Salinger resigned, giving notice to the President on the afternoon of March 19 and leaving the White House at the close of that same business day. He did this in order to run for the Democratic nomination for U.S. Senator from California in place of the ailing Clair Engle.

The two press secretaries were as different as day and night. Salinger was colorful and outgoing. Reedy was quiet and unobtrusive. He had been associated with Mr. Johnson since 1951 in various ways, but the call to this new function was so sudden he was routed out of a hospital bed. The swap brought no essential change in the functioning of the White House news room except to replace a flamboyant secretary with a quiet one.

In his first weeks in the White House, the new President conferred with pundit Walter Lippmann at the latter's home. He also had luncheon dates with a variety of journalists—including, for example, two old friends, Gerald Griffin and Phil Potter, of the Baltimore Sun. His first news conference was held December 7, a Saturday, on the sixteenth day of his incumbency. It grew out of what was to have been a routine briefing for two dozen correspondents by Secretary Salinger. Unexpectedly they found themselves ushered into the President's office where they remained for half an hour, with coffee served by Navy mess attendants. Photographs were permitted but no tape recorders or filming equipment. Reportedly the President made a slip about the orbital vehicle Dyno-Soar that was quickly corrected by Defense Secretary Robert S. McNamara; Secretary Salinger asked the reporters to forget the President's remarks on the subject and to use those of Secretary McNamara.[2]

Johnson's second news conference, also impromptu, occurred December 18. It was described as "a surprise call to the reporters who happened to be there around noon that day." The President answered seventeen questions, including some at length, but also with several off-the-record remarks. On December 21, another Saturday, he led a score of reporters on a tour of the White House including part of the private quarters. On Christmas Eve four women reporters got a cordial reception, along with Mr. Johnson's personal comments on life as chief executive, a tour of the mansion, and autographed pictures of the Johnson family.

Then followed the colorful week at the L.B.J. ranch. This gave the President a fresh excuse for entertaining the visiting correspondents. Again he called an impromptu news conference and then, somewhat to Mrs. Johnson's dismay, took about fifty of the visitors through the entire ranch house. Such a tour had been scheduled for December 27; on that day some 200 news media representatives descended on the ranch, coming by bus from Austin. A barbecue followed, in the midst of which the President chose to make some announcements. While the reporters were still eating, a podium was set up with a microphone on two bales of hay and Mr. Johnson, after taking over from Secretary Salinger, ticked off a series of announcements. He also answered about ten questions. The entire affair lasted twenty minutes.[3] It was doubtful whether any previous administration, even that of Franklin D. Roosevelt, had achieved so much informality on so great a scale in so short a time.

Back in Washington, the President continued the informal type of news conferences. One byproduct of Saturday news conferences was prominent headlines in the Sunday newspapers. But whether this was by design or accident was not clear Through former Press Secretary James C. Hagerty, of American Broadcasting Company, it was proposed that the television networks be permitted to equip the so-called Fish Room in the White House for news conferences. There was no immediate response to this but in time a permanent television facility was arranged for, the cost being shared by the major networks.

At the January 25 news conference the President had some direct comments about his kind of news conferences. After several announcements, he said, "Don't run out of here if you have questions you want to ask. Ask them. I will answer them. This is not a quickie news conference. I don't know what you call a formal one. I guess I ought to wear a white tie. I came to work this morning and I didn't think it was formal. I just thought I was supposed to be here, and if you are all here, I will give you anything I know at any time."

He remarked that some of them evidently felt that he did not see enough of them individually. He said he had seen thirty or forty reporters who had "asked to come in on special things they wanted to do." He added that he tried "to see all of them I can with my

schedule and I am very happy with them. I never enjoy anything
more than polite, courteous, fair, judicious reporters, and I think all
of you qualify." [4] With two of his aides, the President that week visited
the home of Marguerite Higgins, *Newsday* correspondent.

Instead of using his office, the President held his February 1 news
conference in the projection room in the east side of the White House.
More than 100 correspondents, Secret Service men, photographers
and others crowded into the room which had about ninety chairs. The
standing-room-only situation led to a direct question. The President
was asked why, when larger facilities were available, the conference
was held in "a cramped little room." His answer was three-fold: he
thought it would be "ample to take care of your needs," the correspondents had wanted a news conference that week, and it was "much
more convenient to come here at the time I could come."

Three months after Mr. Johnson took office an article in *Editor* &
Publisher asserted flatly that "The 'honeymoon' is over between L.B.J.
and the press." This was open to some doubt as developments of succeeding months were to show. Caryl Rivers, the writer of the article,
quoted an unnamed reporter as saying "President Johnson doesn't
spend as much time fraternizing with reporters these days, and he's
not as ebullient when he's thrown in with us as he used to be. If
someone says something he doesn't like, he's hurt personally by it."
To this Press Secretary Salinger observed that whatever the President did with the press he could not win.

As to Johnson's press relations, Rivers' article continued, some
reporters described them as in a "state of flux." One correspondent,
also unidentified, said the conferences had "good aspects. They're
a lot more informal and less of a production than Kennedy's were.
But often we're not prepared, and of course it's very unfair to the
small bureaus who can't keep a man at the White House all the time."
Yet other correspondents preferred the informal conferences since
they felt that the President was likely to say more without television
cameras staring at him.[5] In the same issue, in reply to a query, former
President Truman commented that he neither approved nor disap-
proved of Johnson's news policies and emphasized that "Each President decides for himself how he wants to maintain his relations with
the press and there is no other procedure."

Finally, on February 29, another Saturday, President Johnson held
his first televised news conference. It was his 100th day in office.
This time the correspondents and camera men had 24-hour notice.
The place was a State Department conference room which seats 400;

305 newsmen were present. The President remained seated during the conference. A composite opinion of participating newsmen, according to *Editor & Publisher,* gave the President "a grade of 'passing to fair' on his performance." One criticism was that he spoke too slowly in contrast to the Kennedy rapid-fire technique.

As on other occasions, Mr. Johnson was asked about his press relations. He stated that he would have briefings by the Press Secretary "at least twice a day, and make available all the information that can be made available to the press. From time to time I will see individual members of the press about press business and I may see some of my particular friends socially occasionally—I hope without too much criticism. I know of nothing in the President's job that is more important than being held accountable to the people, explaining to the people the reasons for his actions . . ."[6]

On yet another Saturday, March 21, a press briefing was scheduled for noon. But it was 1:50 before Secretary Reedy called the hungry and somewhat unhappy correspondents into his office. There were a few mild gibes as Reedy got on with an announcement. Then the connecting door to the President's office opened and Mr. Johnson asked whether it was "all right with you all if I monitor George's press conference?" Out of this grew another impromptu news conference in which the President discussed diplomatic difficulties with Panama. Some correspondents were said to be annoyed because it was known that Lady Barbara Ward Jackson, an English writer, had been visiting with the President for an hour and a half previous.[7]

Formal and informal news conferences were not Mr. Johnson's only contact with the press. On April 20, 1964, for example, he addressed the annual luncheon of the Associated Press in New York City. He used the occasion to announce to his audience of 1700 that he had ordered a substantial reduction in U.S. production of enriched uranium. He disclosed further that Nikita Khrushchev, the Soviet leader, had agreed to make a similar announcement on behalf of Russia simultaneously in Moscow.

In April and May the President addressed two small editorial groups at the White House. One was the eighth National Foreign Policy Conference for Editors and Broadcasters held on April 20-21. Several hundred editors and radio-television newsmen braced themselves against a damp, chill wind in the White House rose garden as they heard a Johnson plea to back his "War on Poverty." The President spoke at some length, followed by questions and answers, and a handshake for those present. In all, Mr. Johnson answered fourteen questions. One had to do with his relations with the press. "The press does its job as it sees it," the President replied, "and I try to do mine the same way. So far as I know, we are both working reasonably well together." [8]

On May 12, he spoke at the spring meeting of the Newspaper Farm Editors Association in the cabinet room. Other correspondents and photographers were present. Afterward one of the farm editors' group asked Mr. Johnson whether he would talk to them alone. He acquiesced and led the way to his office where he chatted with them for a quarter of an hour. Then they took him up on an invitation for a brief personally conducted tour of the second floor of the White House, telling them anecdotes about some of its appointments. [9]

Other members of the President's immediate official family took part in the the American Society of Newspaper Editors meeting April 16 to 18 in the capital. Among them were Attorney General Robert Kennedy and Press Secretary George Reedy. The latter told the editors that any efforts to manage news would "not only be wrong, but futile. Nothing could be more deadly than giving only one side, one view." But he added that he could and would present the viewpoint of the administration without trying to "manage" the flow of information from the White House. [10] On the question of the formal news conference, used widely under Kennedy and Eisenhower, versus the more frequent informal type of news conferences under Johnson, the press secretary was unwilling to commit himself. He conceded, however, that the latter type created difficulties for television and for the smaller news bureaus.

Merriman Smith, the Pulitzer prize-winning correspondent, favored the Johnson policy on news conferences he told the annual meeting of United Press International April 20 in New York City. In his opinion the President was serving himself and the nation better with his method of holding news conferences so far than by scheduled appearances which Smith said often proved artificial. The correspondents, in turn, he added, were covering the White House better than if the President let himself be forced into a television format. The nonscheduled news conferences, Smith noted, took more manpower but, he added, "we'll handle it." He commented also that the President and his staff were "extremely sensitive" to all that was written about them. [11] This had been true also under Mr. Kennedy.

Some days earlier at a National Press Club party honoring Secretary Reedy the President dropped by at the last minute. In the days preceding he had been under newspaper and other criticism for his recent fast automobile driving in Texas during the Easter holiday. Mr. Johnson paid tribute to Mr. Reedy. In an indirect reference to the fast driving issue he told the audience of 600, "you're not bad fellows at night." [42]

By the end of his first six months in the White House, some concern began to be expressed over whether the President was not being over-exposed. Mr. Johnson had appeared in and out of Washington under all sorts of conditions. Using Air Force One, in combination with helicopters and automobiles, he had covered an incredible amount of ground. Twice in a matter of days he had been to the New York World's Fair.

As Douglas Kiker, of the Washington staff of the New York *Herald Tribune,* phrased it, the President's problem was "How much news about the personal activity of Lyndon B. Johnson can the public take without being bored?" On the whole, public reaction to this heavy exposure seemed to be favorable even though some of it left a "corny" taste.

At his somewhat circusy news conference of May 6 on the White House lawn, with the wives and children of correspondents present, Mr. Johnson was asked directly whether he felt that "over-exposure is a problem of your Presidency." The President explained, in reply, that he strove "to please . . . I always want to remain accessible." To this he added the hope that "the press will never be critical of me for being over-accessible."

The consensus seemed to be that he was not. Yet it was pointed out that on his second appearance May 9 at the World's Fair only the New York City newspapers for the most part gave front page prominence to his impromptu news conference. Kiker called this "an unprecedented situation." By implication this smacked of over-exposure. But Kiker cited another point. This was that the President "holds news conferences all the time, but in them, he uses up valuable time to pump tired old themes and to announce trivia, and his answers to substantive questions generally are unresponsive."

Kiker noted also that in the weeks just prior to mid-May, Mr. Johnson had made as much news "by his personal conduct as he has by his conduct in office—maybe more." Among the items were his dancing, his pulling the ears of his dogs, his fast driving in Texas, his conducting of personal tours of the White House grounds, and his return to public wearing of a Texas rancher's hat. In Kiker's words, "He finally has started acting naturally . . ." [13]

In a review of the first half year of the Johnson regime, Douglas B.

Cornell, a veteran member of the Washington staff of the Associated Press, also had some observations about over-exposure and related matters. He, too, touched on the Johnson sensitivity. "He is sensitive to stories or events," Cornell wrote, "that reflect unfavorably on him. And he is sensitive about being called sensitive."

Cornell went on: "In six months, Johnson's skittishness about news conferences has disappeared, to the extent that he has held three in one week, conducted a roving conference on a seven-lap tour of the backyard, and turned another into a punch and cookies outing for wives and children of reporters." But, like Kiker, Cornell was of the opinion that "Lately, though, there have been too much of presidential appearances and exposure. News conferences have slacked off and the President's official busy schedule is less jammed." [14] Where Mr. Johnson had held news conferences on May 4, May 6 and May 9, he had none in the next thirteen days.

Subsequently President Johnson showed repeatedly that he could be flexible in his dealings with the White House correspondents, that he preferred informality to formality, that he could be somewhat unpredictable in this area, and that innovations would continue. But he proved also that the Presidential news conference, whether formal or informal, was a fixed part of the machinery of the executive branch of the government. For more than half a century the American public, to paraphrase a line from the song in "My Fair Lady," had grown increasingly accustomed to its face. As the 1964 election drew closer Mr. Johnson held frequent news conferences. Politically and administratively this was desirable from his viewpoint because of the obvious advantages the news conferences gave him in keeping himself and his views continually before the public.

REFERENCES

II

1. The sessions of the Senate were secret until 1794. By long-standing rule both Houses retain the right to hold secret sessions, but this is rarely done.
2. Details taken, in the main, from files of the New York *Herald Tribune*.

III

1. *Editor & Publisher*, April 21, 1945, p. 9.
2. "Capital Writers Ired by News Blockades," James J. Butler, *Editor & Publisher*, March 30, 1946, p. 28.
3. Columbus *Citizen*, Dec. 6, 1950.
4. As quoted in the New York *Herald Tribune*, Dec. 7, 1950.
5. *Ibid.*, Dec. 9, 1950.
6. Memorandum with personal letter from well-known head of a Washington bureau to author, May 1951.
7. *Editor & Publisher*, Dec. 18, 1948, p. 42.
8. *Editor & Publisher*, April 26, 1947, pp. 10, 109.
9. *Ibid.*, p. 109.   10. 498 papers.   11. 117 papers.   12. 79 papers.
13. *Editor & Publisher*, Sept. 11, 1948, p. 5.
14. *Ibid.*, Oct. 30, 1948, p. 11.   15. *Ibid.*, Nov. 6, 1948, p. 32.
16. *Ibid.*, p. 5. But Arthur Krock, also of the New York *Times*, and a veteran Washington observer, disagrees. "The newspaper political analysts and reporters were misled," he insists, because "the managing politicians in numerous states, whose business it is to know election trends in their areas and who exist chiefly for that purpose, were all wrong, and it was on their private estimates that the reporters were wrong. When the Democratic leaders in states with nearly 200 electoral votes privately predict that their states are going Republican, it is ridiculous to expect non-professionals, such as reporters to know better." Letter to author, June 7, 1951.
17. *Ibid.*
18. New York *Times*, Feb. 17, 1950. In the interview, to quote the *Times* headline, Mr. Truman saw "Man's Better Nature Bringing Peace to the World," *ibid.*, Feb. 15, 1951. According to *Editor & Publisher* Grove Patterson, editor of the Toledo *Blade*, also had an exclusive interview with Mr. Truman July 13, 1948. *Ibid.*, July 24, 1948, p. 34.
19. New York *Herald Tribune*, Dec. 8, 1950.
20. Personal letter to author.   21. Personal letter to author.

IV

1. Columbus *Citizen*, June 6, 1951.
2. New York *Times*, June 8, 1951.   3. *Ohio State Journal*, Aug. 3, 1951.
4. *Ibid.*, Aug. 10, 1951.   5. Columbus *Dispatch*, Sept. 26, 1951.
6. *Ibid.*, Sept. 28, 1951.   7. Sept. 30, 1951.   8. Sept. 27, 1951.
9. Sept. 27, 1951.   10. New York *Herald Tribune*, Oct. 21, 1951.

11. Columbus *Dispatch*, Oct. 12, 1951.   12. Cincinnati *Times-Star*, Oct. 4, 1951.
13. Columbus *Dispatch*, Oct. 8, 1951.   14. *Ibid.*
15. Cleveland *Plain Dealer*, Nov. 30, 1951.
16. Columbus *Citizen*, Nov. 30, 1951.   17. Toledo *Blade*, Nov. 30, 1951.
18. Associated Press file, Dec. 13, 1951.
19. Cleveland *Plain Dealer*, Dec. 16, 1951.
20. New York *Herald Tribune*, Dec. 14, 1951.
21. The publishers have generously given permission to quote from it here.
22. William Hillman, *Mr. President*, p. 2.
23. *Ibid.*, p. 47.   24. *Ibid.*, p. 49.   25. *Ibid.*, pp. 131-2.
26. *Ibid.*, pp. 133-4.   27. *Ibid.*, p. 149.   28. *Ibid.*, p. 219.   29. *Ibid.*, p. 229.
30. *Ibid.*, p. 23.   31. Cleveland *Plain Dealer*, Jan. 25, 1952.
32. New York *Herald Tribune*, Jan. 6, 1952.
33. New York *Times*, March 16, 1952.   34. Columbus *Dispatch*, March 20, 1952.
35. Youngstown *Vindicator*, April 20, 1952.
36. Columbus *Dispatch*, April 25, 1952.
37. Cincinnati *Times-Star*, April 18, 1952.   38. Detroit *Free Press*, May 4, 1952.
39. Associated Press file, April 24, 1952.   40. Columbus *Citizen*, April 24, 1952.
41. *Ibid.*, May 22, 1952.   42. Columbus *Dispatch*, June 5, 1952.
43. *Ohio State Journal*, June 19, 1952.
44. New York *Herald Tribune*, July 27, 1952.
45. *Ohio State Journal*, Aug. 28, 1952.
46. New York *Herald Tribune*, Sept. 12, 1952.   47. *Ibid.*, but separate story.
48. *Ibid.*, Nov. 6, 1952.   49. *Ibid.*, Nov. 21, 1952.   50. *Ibid.*, Dec. 5, 1952.
51. Associated Press file, Dec. 11, 1952.   52. Cleveland *Plain Dealer*, Dec. 12, 1952.
53. New York *Herald Tribune*, Dec. 19, 1952.   54. *Ibid.*, Dec. 27, 1952.
55. *Ibid.*, Dec. 29, 1952.   56. New York *Times*, Dec. 28, 1952.
57. New York *Herald Tribune*, Dec. 31, 1952.
58. Columbus *Dispatch*, Jan. 2, 1953.
59. Unofficial transcript, New York *Times*, Feb. 16, 1953; there are minor variations
between the *Times* and *Herald Tribune* accounts.
60. Detroit *Free Press*, Feb. 15, 1953.

V

1. Columbus *Dispatch* (AP), Jan. 3, 1953.   2. Jan. 24, 1953.
3. She held her first news conference March 11, 1953, with about 100 men and
women reporters present.
4. In his "Today and Tomorrow," Feb. 2, 1953.
5. *Time*, the New York *Times*, and the New York *Herald Tribune* gave the number
as 294, the A.P. as 256.
6. New York *Herald Tribune* transcript, Feb. 18, 1953.
7. New York *Times*, Feb. 18, 1953.
8. New York *Herald Tribune*, Feb. 22, 1953.
9. John S. Knight, "The Editor's Notebook," Detroit *Free Press*, Feb. 22, 1953.
10. *Ohio State Journal* (AP), Feb. 26, 1953.   11. *Ibid.*, April 3, 1953.
12. Detroit *Free Press*, April 19, 1953.
13. From New York *Herald Tribune* transcript, May, 15, 1953.

14. New York *Herald Tribune*, May 29, 1953.   15. *Ibid.*, June 5, 1953.

16. Columbus *Dispatch* (AP), Oct. 1, 1953.

17. New York *Daily News*, Oct. 1, 1953.

18. New York *Herald Tribune*, Oct. 22, 1953.   19. *Ibid.*, Oct. 23, 1953.

20. Associated Press report, Oct. 27, 1953.

21. New York *Herald Tribune*, Nov. 5, 1953.

22. Columbus *Dispatch* (AP), Nov. 6, 1953.

23. *Nieman Reports*, Jan. 1954, pp. 41-3.   24. Nov. 16, 1953.

25. New York *Times*, Nov. 15, 1953.   26. Nov. 18, 1953.

27. Columbus *Dispatch*, Dec. 17, 1953.

28. Radio-Television News Directors Association *Bulletin*, VIII, No. 1, Jan. 1954.

29. Columbus *Citizen*, Jan. 15, 1954.

30. New York *Herald Tribune*, Jan. 29, 1954.

31. *Ohio State Journal* (AP), Jan. 28, 1954.   32. March 11, 1954.

33. *Ohio State Journal*, March 18, 1954.

34. New York *Herald Tribune*, April 1, 1954.

35. Columbus *Citizen* (UP), April 23, 1954.

36. New York *Herald Tribune*, April 26, 1954.   37. *Ibid.*, April 30, 1954.

38. *Ibid.*, May 2, 1954.   39. New York *Herald Tribune*, May 20, 1954.

40. Columbus *Dispatch* (AP), May 28, 1954.

41. New York *Herald Tribune*, May 30, 1954.

42. Akron *Beacon Journal*, June 13, 1954.

43. Columbus *Dispatch*, June 27, 1954.   44. Columbus *Citizen*, July 5, 1954.

45. Columbus *Dispatch* (AP), June 2, 1954.

46. *Ohio State Journal*, July 28, 1954.

47. New York *Herald Tribune*, Aug. 5, 1954.

48. New York *Herald Tribune*, Aug. 8, 1954.   49. *Ibid.*, Aug. 13, 1954.

50. Quoted by *Time*, Aug. 23, 1954.   51. Oct. 28, 1954.

52. Transcript, New York *Herald Tribune*, Nov. 4, 1954.

53. New York *Herald Tribune*, Dec. 6, 1954.

54. Columbus *Citizen*, Dec. 27, 1954.

55. *Ohio State Journal* (AP), Jan. 27, 1955.   56. AP report, Jan. 19, 1955.

57. *Ibid.*   58. Jan. 21, 1955.   59. *Editor & Publisher*, Jan. 15, pp. 8-9.

VI

1. Cf. Pollard, *The Presidents and the Press*, pp. 768-69.

2. *Ibid.*, p. 833.   3. *Ibid.*, p. 835.

4. J. R. Wiggins, chairman of the American Society of Newspaper Editors freedom of information committee, praised the White House staff for keeping the public fully informed on the President's illness, Akron *Beacon Journal*, Oct. 16, 1955.

5. Cincinnati *Enquirer*, Oct. 14, 1955.

6. Associated Press story, Columbus *Dispatch*, Oct. 26, 1955.

7. Article by Marvin Arrowsmith, veteran Associated Press White House reporter, in the Denver *Post*, Aug. 17, 1955.   8. United Press story, Oct. 20, 1955.

9. New York *Herald Tribune*, Dec. 22, 1955.

10. *Cf. Time*, Dec. 26, 1955, p. 51.   11. *Ibid.*

12. New York *Herald Tribune*, Dec. 13, 1955.

VII

1. New York *Herald Tribune,* May 12, 1960.
2. Columbus *Citizen-Journal,* May 13, 1960.
3. New York *Herald Tribune,* May 12, 1960.
4. *Editor & Publisher,* Jan. 21, 1961, p. 6.
5. *Ibid.,* p. 15.   6. *Ibid.*
7. New York *Herald Tribune,* Jan. 19, 1961.
8. New York *Times,* Jan. 19, 1961.
9. *Ibid.*   10. *Ibid.*
11. Columbus *Dispatch,* Jan. 12, 1961.
12. New York *Herald Tribune,* Jan. 10, 1961.

VIII

1. P. 6.
2. *Editor & Publisher,* April 22, 1961, p. 15; *Ibid.,* Nov. 30, 1963, p. 19.
3. *Ibid.,* May 6, 1961, pp. 12, 68.
4. *Ibid.,* Nov. 30, 1963, p. 19.
5. *Ibid.,* 64   6. *Ibid.*   7. *Ibid.*   8. *Ibid.*
9. From U.P.I. report, December 7, 1962.
10. The source for much of what follows in this portion, unless otherwise attributed, is an unpublished M.A. thesis, "The Presidential Press Secretary," by Douglas M. Bloomfield, Ohio State University, 1963. Bloomfield obtained much of his information first hand but on condition that it be anonymous.
11. July 28, 1962.   12. *Editor & Publisher,* Dec. 2, 1961.   13. April 8, 1963.
14. William S. White, in *Harper's,* April 1962, p. 92 ff.
15. *Nieman Reports,* December 1962.
16. At Sigma Delta Chi convention, Tulsa, Okla., November 1962.
17. *Editor & Publisher,* March 30, 1963, p. 133.
18. April 8, 1963.
19. Based on letter from Salinger to author, Oct. 31, 1963. The figures do not include state newspaper group luncheons.
20. Quotations and excerpts that follow are from the *Congressional Record* and by courtesy of *Fortune* magazine and the authors.
21. Cited by John C. Colburn in the 1962 John Peter Zenger address at the University of Arizona.
22. August 28, 1962.
23. From copy of letter supplied to author.   24. Sept. 8, 1963.

IX

1. Columbus *Dispatch,* May 12, 1964.
2. *Editor & Publisher,* December 14, 1963, pp. 11, 86.
3. *Ibid.,* January 4, 1964, pp. 9-10.   4. *Ibid.,* February 1, 1964, pp. 9-10.
5. *Ibid.,* February 22, 1964, pp. 17, 52.   6. *Ibid.,* March 7, 1964, p. 57.
7. *Ibid.,* March 28, 1964, p. 14.   8. *Ibid.,* May 16, 1964, p. 36.

9. Columbus *Dispatch,* May 18, 1964.

10. *Editor & Publisher,* April 25, 1964 p. 19.

11. *Ibid.*   12. *Ibid.,* April 11, 1964, p. 15.

13. New York *Herald Tribune,* May 14, 1964.

14. Columbus *Dispatch,* May 22, 1964.

REFERENCES